A VISUAL HISTORY OF COSTUME

The Nineteenth Century

VANDA FOSTER

B T BATSFORD LTD, LONDON
DRAMA BOOK PUBLISHERS,
NEW YORK

Acknowledgments

Printed in Great Britain by
Butler & Tanner Ltd
Frome, Somerset
for the publishers
B. T. Batsford Ltd
4 Fitzhardinge Street
London W1H 0AH

ISBN 0 7134 4095 3

Published in USA by
Drama Book Publishers
821 Broadway
New York,   New York 10003

ISBN 0 89676 079 0

I would like to thank all the institutions and collectors
mentioned in the List of Illustrations for supplying the
photographs for this book. I am particularly grateful to
Miss Judith Prendergast of the National Portrait
Gallery, and to Miss Jane Tozer and Miss Sarah Levitt
of the Gallery of English Costume, Manchester, for their
invaluable assistance in selecting material. I would also
like to thank Dr Aileen Ribeiro of the Courtauld
Institute of Art, and Timothy Auger, Clare Sunderland
and Belinda Baker of Batsford for making this book
possible. Finally, I am indebted to Veronica Heley for
her advice on magazine illustrations, and for all her
practical and moral support.

For Simon and Sam

Contents

Preface

A Visual History of Costume is a series devised for those who need reliable, easy-to-use reference material on the history of dress.

The central part of each book is a series of illustrations, in black-and-white and colour, taken from the time of the dress itself. They include oil paintings, engravings, woodcuts and line drawings. By the use of such material, the reader is given a clear idea of what was worn and how, without the distortions and loss of detail which modern drawings can occasionally entail.

Each picture is captioned in a consistent way, under the headings, where appropriate, 'Head', 'Body' and 'Accessories'; the clothes are not just described, but their significance explained. The reader will want to know whether a certain style was fashionable or unfashionable at a certain time, usual or unusual – such information is clearly and consistently laid out. The illustrations are arranged in date order, and the colour illustrations are numbered in sequence with the black-and-white, so that the processes of change can be clearly followed.

The pictures will be all the better appreciated if the reader has at least some basic overall impression of the broad developments in dress in the period concerned, and the Introduction is intended to provide this.

Technical terms have been kept to a reasonable minimum. Many readers will use these books for reference, rather than read them straight through from beginning to end. To explain every term each time it is used would have been hopelessly repetitive, and so a Glossary has been provided. Since the basic items of dress recur throughout the book, a conventional, full Index would have been equally repetitive; therefore the Glossary has been designed also to act as an Index; after each entry the reader will find the numbers of those illustrations which show important examples of the item concerned.

List of Illustrations

Introduction

It was in the nineteenth century that fashion, in terms of an interest in dress and its changing styles, became a predominantly female concern. From the early years of the century, the two sexes began to adopt diverging roles in society. In a rapidly changing social order, the masculine ideal became one of stolid integrity and economic reliability, expressed in safe, conservative styles of clothing, in discreet and sombre colours. The female, on the other hand, was seen as a mere dependent, a decorative accessory, who could display the family wealth and social status in the quality and fashionableness of her dress. Thus, while men's clothing became increasingly standardized over the century, women's demonstrated a wide variety of styles, which changed more rapidly than in any previous period.

This variety in dress was made possible by the greater buying power of the growing *nouveaux riches*, coupled with the greater diffusion of information on fashion which resulted from improved communications. It was further promoted by the major technical developments in clothing production which were a feature of the nineteenth century. As early as 1808, Heathcote's invention of a Bobbin Net machine introduced a cheaper alternative to hand-made lace. In the 1830s, the import of the Jacquard loom into Great Britain revolutionized the production of woven silks. In 1845 in the United States of America Elias Howe invented a sewing machine, a version of which was soon widely sold in Britain, marketed by the American firm of Singer. From the mid-1860s, traditional hand sewing was replaced almost entirely by machine work. There was a rapid increase in the use of paper patterns, which received a further boost when Butterick's opened an English branch in 1873, while further developments of the sewing machine led to the greater mechanization of clothing and footwear trades, and the growth of ready-to-wear. The year 1856 saw Perkins' discovery of the first aniline dyes, and in 1892 the first synthetic silk was created, forerunner of the modern range of man-made fibres.

Yet despite these technical advances, there were many constants in the history of nineteenth-century dress. Even in women's clothing, certain standards were never challenged. Dresses were always shaped and supported by whaleboned stays and petticoats. Sleeveless dresses were unthinkable during the day. Hats or bonnets were essential out of doors, and skirts, despite their variety of shapes, never rose much above the ankle. When, in the early 1850s, the American reformer Mrs Amelia Bloomer tried to introduce a form of trousers for women, she found that, for the majority, she was way ahead of her time.

In the nineteenth century changes in fashion were limited and progressive. Waistlines rose and skirts expanded over a number of years. New styles generally took shape quite steadily, reaching an extreme form from which they then reverted more rapidly, giving way to a new emphasis, and the beginning of another fashion. Each new silhouette was created by its own substructure, in the form of stays, petticoats, crinoline or bustle, and individual garments and accessories were all adapted to create the total look of the moment. Thus, when presented with a chronological survey, it is usually possible to chart these modifications, and to pinpoint an outfit on the line of progress from one fashion to another.

In women's dress, in the first two decades of the century, the general look was high-waisted and narrow, owing much to the general wave of neo-classicism. Hair was short and tousled 'à la Titus', or long and bunched in ringlets on the crown, in the style of ancient Greece. Soft white cotton muslins were almost universal for day and evening wear, imitating the clinging draperies seen in antique marble statues. The *avant-garde* who followed fashion to its extremes were reputed to have renounced all forms of underwear in the attempt to recreate the classical silhouette. The more conservative majority, however, still retained the basic linen chemise, with stays and a single petticoat, finding, indeed, that longer stays were necessary if the average figure was to conform to the sinuous ideal.

With low, drawstring necks, or cross-over bodices, these muslin dresses were usually made with an apron front; the upper third of the skirt was slit at the sides, the front lifting up to fasten with ties round the waist. In many cases the bodice front was attached, and also lifted up to fasten to the shoulders by means of pins or cotton-covered buttons. In the early years, bodice, skirt and short sleeves were full and gathered, giving a softly rounded silhouette, but after 1805 a higher waistline, long, narrow sleeves and a less gathered skirt created a more rigid vertical line.

Headwear was small and neat, but included a wide range of styles and trimmings. Outerwear either followed the line of the dress in fitted spencers and pelisses, or provided additional draperies in the form of Indian shawls, enveloping cloaks and mantles and loose tunics. Footwear was flat, or made with a minute wedge heel; half boots were usual for outdoor wear, and simple kid or silk slippers for indoors, sometimes with ribbon ties across the instep in imitation of Roman sandals.

Even at its purest, this neo-classical style often included motifs from other cultures, such as Egyptian palm designs, or Elizabethan ruffs, but from 1815, the year of the long-awaited peace with France, Romantic influences began to dominate. Waists rose still higher, and the width across the bust was further emphasized by puffed sleeves. Hems were also raised, and were stiffened by flounces or padded ribbons, while skirts were now gored, producing an unmistakable A-line. By 1817, dresses and pelisses were encrusted with vandyke frills and rouleaux, the general cone-shaped outline completed by a tall-crowned, wide-brimmed bonnet, topped with ostrich plumes. Softly draped white muslins were being replaced by stiffer, printed cottons and light-coloured silks, while for evening lustrous satins were veiled by over-dresses of paler net, producing shimmering pastel shades.

In 1820 the waistline began to drop, reaching its natural level by 1827. Longer, fitted bodices were now fastened at the back by means of hooks and eyes of flattened brass wire, the usual method until the introduction of front-fastening jacket bodices in the 1840s. Sleeves and hems widened, and bonnet brims flattened or dipped in front, echoing the same line. By the middle of the decade, bonnets with soft crowns and wide, flat brims were virtually indistinguishable from hats.

By the late 1820s, female fashions were angular and exuberant. Width was given to the face by sausage-shaped curls at each temple, on top of which rested huge cartwheel hats, their crowns sprouting trimmings of grass, flowers, feathers and stiff ribbon bows. From 1824 evening hairstyles echoed this general shape in the Apollo knot, a virtual parody of the classical knot of curls, consisting of upstanding loops of plaited hair, decorated with feathers or skewered with Glauvina pins. Even daytime caps were large, a positive halo of stiffened muslin and ribbons. Dresses were equally expansive, with huge gigot sleeves, distended by down-filled pads or cane hoops. Tiny waists were tightly laced into heavily boned stays, and wide, gored skirts, supported by stiff cotton petticoats, were gathered at the back over flounced cotton bustles. Outerwear was adapted to the new shape. Spencers would have looked top-heavy with such large sleeves, but fitted pelisses followed the new line, while shawls and mantles were all-enveloping, and wide capes and pelerines gave additional emphasis to the shoulders. Even footwear reflected the angular silhouette, with toes becoming square by the end of the decade.

From 1830, steadily inflating sleeves and skirts began to billow and sag like overblown roses, and the centre of gravity began its descent towards the hemline. Hats and bonnets grew smaller, their upturned brims framing the face in a narrow oval. Wide, straight necklines cut across the points of the shoulders so that the huge balloon-like sleeves were set in low on the arm, and found their maximum width around the level of the elbow. Waistlines were still dropping, and from 1828, the downward movement was emphasized by a V-shape of pleated folds on the bodice front. From the same year a new full skirt was created by pleating straight widths of fabric to the tiny waist. For these softly draped forms, plain lightweight silks, or fine, flower-printed wool or cotton muslins were the popular fabrics.

In 1836 the sleeve had reached its ultimate width, and began to collapse. Initially, the top was pleated or gathered to the upper arm, and then the lower sleeve narrowed too, leaving only a puff at the elbow. By 1840, this too had disappeared, and the billowing curves were finally replaced by a new silhouette, the dominant shape of the 1840s, base on the Gothic arch. Its narrow apex was a neat, smooth hairstyle, in which the front hair was sleeked down from a centre parting, and looped over the ears, or, particularly for evening, draped in long side ringlets, and wound into a knot on the crown. By the end of the decade, this knot had slipped down towards the back of the neck, and all emphasis was on the sides of the face. Bonnets followed the same line. From 1838 a tubular shape appeared, the crown continuous with the brim, and throughout the 1840s the brim curved downwards at the sides, demurely enclosing the face and hiding the profile.

As sleeves narrowed, so did the bodice, extending in a long, curved, pointed waistline, stiffened with whalebone and emphasized by trimmings of stiffly pleated folds. Beneath this the skirt grew ever wider, supported by increasing numbers of stiff cotton petticoats, and from 1841 straight widths of fabric were gauged to the waistline, producing a distinctive dome-shape. Hemlines dropped, and footwear lengthened and narrowed, retaining the square toes. The look was one of modesty and reticence. Silks were plain, or figured in gently contrasting tones, and the subtle effects of shot silk were particularly appropriate. Decoration consisted chiefly of stiffly piped seams and flat, pleated draperies on the bodice.

From the mid-1840s, however, there were hints that the silhouette was opening out. By 1844 sleeves were widening below the elbow. Two years later, jacket bodices with basques were appearing, and flounced skirts were becoming increasingly popular. These were to be the dominant features of the 1850s, a decade in which the silhouette became a wide-based triangle, and the hard outlines of the 1840s were softened and blurred.

By 1850 bonnet brims opened more widely round the face and sloped towards the crown. By 1853 they were decreasing in size and had receded to the back of the head, providing only a narrow frame to the face. Wide-brimmed hats were a fashionable alternative for the young and for informal wear. Pagoda sleeves were flared and open at the wrist, softened by full, white, cotton undersleeves. The waistline rose, and basqued bodices blurred its exact position. Skirts grew still wider, with flounces à disposition emphasizing the horizontal line.

Opaque printed muslins, warp-printed silks, draped bodices, flounces, pinked edges and fringe decoration all added to the softer silhouette.

By the mid-1850s it was usual to wear as many as five stiffened petticoats, including one of horsehair, in order to create the fashionable full skirt. In 1856, however, this intolerable burden was relieved by the introduction of a hooped petticoat, not unlike that of the eighteenth century. Called a crinoline, after the horsehair petticoats which it replaced (from the French *crin*, hair), it had an immediate impact on female fashions, and although widely criticized for its impracticalities, it was adopted at almost every level of society. In the decade up to 1868 the crinoline dominated fashion, producing a wide-based triangular silhouette. At its apex, the head was small and neat, the hair smoothed into a neat, round chignon, topped by small hats or tiny, spoon-shaped bonnets. Bodices had fitted sleeves and round waists, slightly above natural level, and skirts, though large, were plain, since flounces (although occasionally worn) appeared excessive. Similarly, plain fabrics were popular, with perhaps a moiré effect, or just a simple pattern of applied braid. Loose-fitting shawls, jackets and mantles were the favourite forms of outerwear.

During the 1860s the crinoline itself was modified in shape. From 1860 it began to flatten at the front, and skirts were gored to follow this line. By 1865 tunic dresses or double skirts gave added emphasis at the back, with the lower skirt extending as a train. In the latter years the framework shrank to a half-crinoline, with half hoops at the back. Finally, by 1868, many crinolines were discarded altogether, leaving a fairly narrow skirt with a train. An alternative was found in the bustle, initially a variant of the half-crinoline, but soon reduced to a large flounced pad of horsehair, tied round the waist. In some cases this was worn on top of a half-crinoline, but by the early 1870s it was worn alone, above flowing, trained petticoats.

The dominant look of the years 1869-74 was frothy and curvaceous. The rising bustle was echoed in a rising chignon, the hair dressed high on the head, with a heavy plait or ringlets at the back, and from 1868, the American fashion for loose back hair was also popular. To accommodate these styles, small hats and bonnets were usually worn with a forward tilt, although after 1873 many were tilted back and sat on top of the chignon. Square necklines were popular, above a high, round waistline, and skirts were flat and narrow at the front, curving in a soft undulating line at the back. From 1872 tapes were attached inside the back of the skirt, holding the upper part in a puff over the bustle. Overskirts, either separate, or attached to the bodice in the polonaise form, were draped to give an apron front and an additional puffed pannier at the back. The whole was encrusted with layers of pleated frills and lace flounces. Now that the sewing machine was making light work of a straight seam, it was as if greater complexities were necessary to prove costly workmanship.

The year 1874 saw the revival of a narrower silhouette. The long cuirass bodice was introduced, fitting snugly over the waist and hips, and necessitating the revival of long stays. Skirts hung flat at the front with gores at the sides, and, in this year, additional tapes were set inside to tie across the back breadths, drawing the front of the skirt more closely to the body. At the same time the bustle grew smaller, and was brought down the skirt, the back fullness extending as a long train. By 1876, according to *The Ladies' Treasury*, skirts were now 'so tight that our sitting and walking are seriously inconvenienced'. Indeed, it was found necessary to reduce the volume of underwear by replacing the separate chemise and drawers with fitted combinations. To emphasize height and slimness, bodice and sleeves were made in contrasting fabrics, coats and mantles were cut to fit closely over the dress, and footwear developed Louis heels of up to two inches.

This narrow style continued into the 1880s, with variations created by the draping of the skirt and overskirt, and by the range of bodices, many of which were cut *en Princesse*, with an attached polonaise overskirt almost as long as the underskirt.

After 1880, the train disappeared except for evening dress, leaving the skirt as a straight tube, smothered in flounces, pleats and ruchings. It was soon replaced by a new form of bustle which dominated the decade, reaching its maximum size by 1887, and finally disappearing in 1889. This bustle was a narrow, angular construction, often made of small steel hoops, and producing a much harder outline than that of the previous decade.

Thus the dominant look of the 1880s was tall and angular. The hair was scraped back from the sides of the face, dressed in a small neat chignon, and, from the middle of the decade, topped by hats and bonnets whose trimmings emphasized their height. Vertical bows, plumes and birds' wings were popular, and the typical style was the hard, tall-crowned, post-boy hat. Collars were tall and military, bodices long, pointed and heavily boned, sleeves narrow, and skirts straight at the front, the bustle forming a shelf-like profile at the back. Formal day and evening dresses had skirts with elaborate and ingenious draperies, but after 1884 the general trend was towards a simpler style. This decade saw the increasing popularity of woollen tailor-made dresses for general day wear, as well as for travelling and sport, and the introduction of the jersey, a simple bodice of knitted wool or silk, worn with a simple skirt.

Although the crinoline had provoked criticism and mockery, the extremes of the late 1870s and early 1880s produced far more drastic reactions. In artistic circles the bright colours, heavy boning and complex draperies of contemporary fashion were compared unfavourably with the plainer forms of mediaeval dress. By the late 1870s, the aesthetes had developed a distinctive style of their own characterized by loose-fitting dresses with puffed sleeves, natural waists and simple trained skirts, in the soft, dull-coloured, oriental silks being popularized by Liberty's. The dress reformers were another vociferous minority group who rejected high fashion, but in their case on the grounds of health and practicality. They too recommended simpler, flowing styles, and many favoured natural woollen fabrics. Even the followers of high fashion sought an alternative to tight-lacing, and found it in the tea-gown, a loose (although still elaborate) garment for the less formal hours between afternoon visiting and dinner.

By 1890 high fashion had adopted many of the recommendations of both aesthetes and dress reformers. Bustles, trains, and complicated skirt draperies had finally been banished in favour of gored A-line skirts. Wool was popular for day wear. In the following decade, matching tailor-made jackets and skirts were even more popular, worn with blouses in an early form of the suit. Separate blouses and skirts were worn on all but the most formal occasions, and in their plainer, more masculine forms were complemented by straw sailor hats and neck ties. The ultimate theft from the male wardrobe came in the form of the wide knickerbockers sometimes worn for cycling. With the liberated 'new woman' of the 1890s, Mrs Bloomer's ideals had been given a reality.

Appearances were deceptive, however. As the informal blouse became more fashionable, it was shaped to the figure by a heavily boned lining and high stiffened collar. Gored skirts gave freedom to the legs but fitted closely to the hips, and the waists of the 1890s were narrower than ever. Finally, from 1890, the sleeve head began to grow, producing by the middle of the decade a revival of the huge, impractical, gigot sleeve of the 1830s. As then, this was offset by the wide hat, narrow waist and gored skirt, with the addition, in this decade, of wide yokes and lapels, and short capes and mantles.

From 1897 came the due reaction to this angular silhouette, and the line began to soften again. The hair was swept up over cushion-like pads to frame the head. Bodices were padded and pouched at the front. Sleeves narrowed, leaving just a puff at the shoulder. Skirts were cut to fit still more closely over the hips, but flared out from below the knee, extending once more as a train at the back, and as lightweight silks and fine wools replaced the heavier fabrics of the early 1890s, the result was a more fluid silhouette. With the introduction of a straight-fronted corset in 1900 which gave the body a characteristic S-bend, the flowing *art nouveau* curves of the Edwardian age were already apparent.

In contrast to these swings of fashion, men's dress was extremely conservative. Post-revolutionary Europe had seen a reaction against the brightly coloured silks and lavish trimmings of the *ancien regime*, so that by 1800 dark cloths and plain styles were the order of the day. Following the tenets of Beau Brummel, the fashionable emphasis was on fit rather than on exciting variations in cut and design. The fancy waistcoat was the only garment in which a sense of colour and pattern could be given free rein. (This was particularly true of the 1840s, the decade in which Charles Dickens, on his American lecture tour, was criticized for wearing bright waistcoats 'somewhat in the flash order'.)

The main developments in men's dress were in the introduction of new garments, and, in the second half of the century, a widening of the available options, with a move towards greater informality. Otherwise, variations in style were subtle and often hard to distinguish, even in the exaggerations of caricatures and fashion plates.

At the beginning of the period, the main coats were the dress tail coat, with its straight front waist, and the less formal morning or riding tail coat, with sloping fronts. From 1816, the nineteenth-century version of the frock coat, with its distinctive straight front edges, made its first appearance, becoming, in the second half of the century, the usual garment for formal day wear, a safe, conservative choice for the respectable middle classes. A short, loose-fitting pilot coat or paletot began life as an overcoat in the 1830s, but soon evolved into a variety of short, informal jackets. Of these, the lounging jacket was soon given the addition of matching waistcoat and trousers, producing, in the 1860s, the early form of the lounge suit. The Norfolk jacket was fashionable country wear in the second half of the century. The 1880s saw the dinner jacket competing with the tail coat for evening wear, and in the 1890s the reefer and blazer jackets evolved from sporting garments as popular leisure wear.

From the late eighteenth century knee breeches were being replaced by tight-fitting, calf- or ankle-length pantaloons, and between 1807 and 1825, these were themselves gradually superseded by trousers. At first these two garments were virtually indistinguishable (hence the American usage of the word pants, the shortened form of pantaloons, as an alternative to trousers). By 1817, however, trousers had lengthened to reach the instep, and in their new form became increasingly popular. By 1850 fly fronts had replaced falls, and in the 1890s front creases and turn-ups became fashionable features. Pantaloons were retained until the middle of the century for evening dress. Similarly, breeches were worn for the rest of the period, but only as full court dress, riding dress, and as unfashionable wear, particularly in the country.

Fine white linen shirts were a status symbol throughout the period, and in the second half of the century, collars, cuffs and fronts were often heavily starched to keep them clean as well as smooth. Initially, collars were attached and swathed in fine linen cravats, but during the 1840s detachable collars appeared, and the cravat narrowed around the neck to be fastened as a loose scarf or large bow at the front. Turn-down collars and shaped neckties finally appeared in the 1860s.

The top hat was worn throughout the century, but again, from the 1850s, a range of less formal styles appeared, including the straw sailor hat, and the hard felt bowler. The soft felt hat with a dented crown, later known as a trilby, appeared in the 1870s, and by the 1890s there was also the harder Homburg, together with a range of caps, helmets and boaters.

Light shoes or pumps were worn with evening dress, but for day wear boots were general. With the advent of trousers, hessians and top boots were replaced by half boots. From 1837 an elastic gusset was a common alternative to front-lacing, while buttons were popular from the 1860s.

Apart from the steady evolution of informal clothes, and their gradual acceptance for more formal occasions, general stylistic changes can also be traced, many of which reflect those of female dress. In the first two decades, the neo-classical ideal was expressed in hair 'à la Titus', and in a narrow, high-waisted silhouette, produced by short-bodied coats and waistcoats, and almost skin-tight pantaloons and trousers. In the 1820s men's coats, like women's dresses, featured full, gathered shoulders and low narrow waists, whose baggier trousers matched widening skirts. In the 1840s men's coats fastened higher to the neck, and waistcoats share not only the same fabrics, colours and patterns as women's dresses, but also their pointed waistlines. Small feet were fashionable for both sexes, and shoes became narrow and square-toed. Waistcoats of the 1860s featured the same higher, rounded waist as dresses, although in other ways men's clothes at this period provided a complete contrast to women's. As the crinoline reached its widest circumference, top hats became tall, narrow 'chimney-pots', coats straightened, and peg-top trousers reversed the wide-based, triangular silhouette of the fashionable female. From then on, men's clothes remained fairly straight and easy-fitting, except for the pointed shoes and high shirt collars of the last two decades, features found also in women's dress.

These were the main developments in male and female fashions, but there were, of course, as many variations in actual dress as there were variations in social gradation, level of income and individual preference. The poorer classes could rarely afford to follow fashion, except perhaps in the general style of the hair, or the trimming of a bonnet. Their clothes were usually home-made and simple, or second-hand and out of date. Alternatively, some sections of working-class society developed their own distinctive garments, such as the countryman's smock, which were outside the influence of high fashion. Even among the middle classes there was often a time lag in the spread of styles from London to the provinces and the countryside, so that the small-town belle might be coveting an outfit already rejected by the *beau monde* of the city. Again, the thrifty might try to update an existing garment, producing an outfit fashionable only in certain features. The elderly frequently clung to the styles of their youth, and different age groups developed different tastes. Caps, for example, were retained by older women long after they were discarded by the young.

Further variations were prompted by the occasion and the time of day, a concept alien to our informal tastes. Morning was the time for household duties, requiring an outfit that was fashionable but fairly plain. More elaborate dress was worn for formal afternoon visiting, although more practical variations were acceptable in the country or for going out walking. The fashionable changed again for dinner, a meal which grew later and more formal as the century progressed, and a further distinction was made between an evening dress suitable for dinner or the theatre, and the still more *décolleté* ball

dress. These distinctions are specified in the illustrations and descriptions found in contemporary fashion magazines, but social variations become apparent only when comparing a number of different sources. Fortunately, there is an enormous range of visual material available for the study of dress in the nineteenth century.

The most obvious source of information is to be found in the garments themselves, for a large number survive in museums and private collections. When studying the fabric, colour and construction of individual items, there is no substitute for actual clothes (although the patterns found in tailoring guides, and after the mid-century in magazines, provide invaluable evidence on cut). For an understanding of the total look, however, shaped by the appropriate underwear, completed by a suitable hairstyle and accessories and worn with the correct posture, one must turn to other forms of documentation.

Of these, the one most widely used is the fashion plate. These charming, often hand-coloured, prints showing figures dressed in the latest styles were issued by contemporary magazines, together with a description of the outfits depicted. They provide for us, as for their oringinal purchasers, a view of the current silhouette, garment and accessories, complete with a description in contemporary terminology. Although depicting actual garments (indeed, some advertised the work of specific dressmakers) these drawings were highly stylized, for they aimed to show the fashionable ideal rather than the reality. (They can be misleading, too, in the depiction of colours, since the range is limited by the print-maker's palette.) There are many histories of dress which use fashion plates to trace the changes in the fashionable ideal. In this book, however, I have tried to redress the balance between ideal and reality by using a variety of visual sources.

The fashion plate had its origins in the early pseudo-scientific surveys of national or occupational dress. This idea was still popular in the nineteenth century, and produced contemporary counterparts in such publications as Pyne's *Costume of Great Britain* (1808), Walker's *Costume of Yorkshire* (1814), and White's *Sketches of Characters* (1818). These series of engravings provide a major source of information on working-class dress, and the variations between different occupations and regions. Some leeway must be granted in their dating, however, for they were often the work of several years, and, in some cases, plates were copied from earlier publications rather than direct from life.

For the middle and upper classes an obvious record is to be found in portraiture. This was still regarded in the nineteenth century as one of the lowest forms of art, and sculptors in particular, used to working on a more grandiose scale, tended to swathe their sitters in classical draperies, or, where appropriate, in civic robes, in order to set them above the mediocrity of everyday life. Nineteenth-century painters, however, although often critical of contemporary dress, were usually content to depict it in their portraits, reserving their grand style for other types of painting. In the hands of a master like

Ingres even a simple pencil sketch can convey a wealth of information on cut, construction and drape, while a full oil painting can express still more about colour, pattern and texture. From the most detailed it is possible to distinguish a satin from a plain-weave silk, or a blonde lace from a linen. Where the painter does attempt to idealize his sitter, however, the usual result is a simplification of hairstyles, draperies and fabric patterns, and a reduction in the range of jewellery and accessories.

In some ways a more accurate rendering of dress is to be found in what Christopher Wood has called 'modern-life' narrative paintings (Christopher Wood, *Victoria Panorama*, 1976). This tradition, dating back to Hogarth, and supported by the Pre-Raphaelite painters, was given a new impetus in the mid-nineteenth century by the work of W.P. Frith. Working from sketches, photographs and posed models, his minutely detailed paintings of contemporary scenes and events were so vast that they often took several years to complete. Nevertheless, his subjects are a valuable source of information on costume, being deliberately chosen to demonstrate a variety of contemporary characters in typical dress.

Even Frith's broad social range was confined to the socially acceptable, however. The widely held view that 'Picture Galleries should be the townman's paradise of refreshment' (Charles Kingsley), did not allow for any representation of the seamier side of life. Only in the 1870s and 1880s did a school of social realism enjoy a brief popularity. Then, painters like Holl, Herkomer and Fildes attempted to depict the real poverty and misery of contemporary life, but even they succumbed to sentiment and melodrama, and their dramatic use of light and shade tends to blur details of dress.

By the 1890s painstaking detail and social realism were almost entirely superseded by the painterly, atmospheric designs of artists influenced by the Impressionists and inspired by the concept of 'art for art's sake'. Even a portrait painter like John Singer Sargent, while brilliantly conveying the character, pose and silhouette of his fashionable sitters, frequently presents their gowns in a shimmering haze of brushstrokes, expressing general effect rather than specific detail.

A complementary viewpoint is provided by the caricaturists, many of whom treated fashion or the fashionable. Through the wit of artists like Gillray, Cruikshank and du Maurier, we are shown not the fashion-plate ideal, but clothing as it was being worn, albeit in an exaggerated form. In his 'Monstrosities of 1818', for example, Cruikshank satirizes the current fashion for shorter skirts. Judging by contemporary fashion plates and portraits, the rise in hemlines was only a matter of an inch or two, and would be almost imperceptible to modern eyes. Only through Cruikshank's exaggeration are we able to recognize a change in style which was obvious to contemporaries.

In the first half of the period such caricatures were usually published and sold individually, but the removal of the paper tax in 1861 produced a flood of illustrated newspapers and journals, providing new outlets for writers, caricaturists and illustrators alike. For the costume historian these publications are a mine of information, not only for the fashion plates, articles, and correspondence on fashion which many of them contain, but also for the wealth of non-fashion illustrations. Here, for the first time, are depicted the subjects of articles, advertisements and popular fiction. Ordinary people, from a variety of social backgrounds, are shown in a variety of situations, and portrayed without the bias of the fashion plate. Outside the magazine illustration, this combination of social range and informality can be found only in the later developments of photography.

Photography is, of course, the other major visual source for the study of Victorian dress. It was in 1837 that Louis Daguerre first produced a clear, permanent photographic image, and within a few years his daguerrotype technique was widely used to create small, mirror-image portraits. Poses were stiff and wooden, for exposures lasted up to a minute, and high costs restricted the process to the middle and upper classes. (Exceptions are found in a few working-class subjects, chosen by photographers like Hill and Adamson for their picturesque qualities.) Although unsophisticated by later standards, these photographs from the 1840s can provide surprisingly clear details of contemporary costume.

The cheaper improved ambrotypes of the 1850s brought portraiture to a wider social range, but the real impetus came with the craze for *cartes de visite* in the 1860s. Portrait photographs of friends, relatives and celebrities, from the royal family downwards, were printed the size of visiting cards and issued by the thousand to avid collectors. Usually studio portraits, with a very limited range of poses and backdrops, they are invaluable for details of fashionable, usually formal, dress.

Although variations on the *cartes de visite* were produced for the rest of the period, by the early 1870s the Anglo-American Edward Muybridge was already experimenting with the photography of moving objects. His discoveries, aided by new technical advances, led to the development of the snapshot. By the late 1880s, the work of Eastman and Walker, and the use of continuous 'American' film, enabled amateurs to capture crowd scenes and outdoor portraits, often without the knowledge of the subject. The latter are unique sources for the study of informal, working-class and occupational dress, although by the very nature of their technique and subject matter they usually lack the fine detail of the studio portrait.

These then, are the main visual sources from which it is possible to study almost every aspect of nineteenth-century dress. There are limitations, however. Underwear, for example, is rarely depicted, except by caricaturists or illustrators of fiction, and in the stylized forms of fashion plates and advertisements. Shoes, gloves, bags and other accessories are rarely shown in any great detail. Except in the work of a few social-realist painters and snapshot photographers later in the century, the poorer classes are usually 'cleaned up' and made acceptably picturesque, so that evidence on their dress may be unreliable. Nevertheless, there is more visual information available on the nineteenth century than on any previous period.

This book aims to show how this evidence may be read and understood, with a view to recognizing and dating the costume portrayed. The illustrations have been chosen to reflect the main developments in fashion. I have included a few examples of non-fashionable dress, however, as a reminder of the constant variations available, and to demonstrate that even these can sometimes reflect fashionable features. The illustrations are drawn from a wide range of sources, bearing in mind that some are more informative, and reproduce more clearly than others. Where a painting has taken a number of years to complete, a suitable date span is quoted. Similarly engravings after popular paintings have been given the date of the original work, since this is more relevent to the costume. In the descriptions, I have tried to use generic terms for the garments (e.g. mantle), since contemporary names (e.g. pardessus) changed so rapidly that they would require constant re-definition. Similarly, fabrics have been described in general terms, since it is now almost impossible to distinguish all the contemporary variations.

If my sin is one of omission, it is because the nineteenth century is so rich a period, both in known varieties of dress and in the range of visual sources for its study.

PLATES & CAPTIONS

20

1 George, Duke of Argyll, 1801
H. Edridge

Note From the 1790s male fashions were noted for their informality and understatement. For all occasions short of full court dress fabrics and styles were simple, colours limited.

Head The hair is short and dishevelled 'a la Titus'.

Body The ruffled linen shirt has a high pointed collar encased in a starched white linen cravat. The formal dress tail coat is of dark woollen cloth; the waistcoat, probably of wool or cotton, has a standing collar. The close-fitting knee-breeches are buttoned and tied at the knee.

Accessories He wears white silk stockings, flat lace-up leather shoes, and short gloves of cotton or fine leather.

2 Princess Augusta, 1802
H. Edridge

Note Although the short hair, bandeau and soft white draperies are overtly classical in inspiration, the skirt is full, supported by a bustle pad at the back waist, and the general effect remains full and rounded, as was fashionable until 1805. Trains were worn with day dresses until 1806.

Head Her short, tousled hair, 'a la Titus' is encircled by a bandeau.

Body The dress is of white muslin, the V-neck indicating a wrap-over front to the bodice. It has a high waist tied with a sash, and a skirt with a short train.

Accessories She wears a black silk mantle, edged with lace; elbow-length gloves of silk or fine kid; pointed shoes with ribbon ties and very low heels; and a necklace with an anchor pendant.

3 Princess Sophia, 1802
H. Edridge

Note For day wear, low necks were often filled in by a handkerchief, chemisette or tucker, and thin fabrics augmented by a variety of shawls, mantles, cloaks, tunics, 'vests' and pelisses.

Head The short tousled hair 'a la Titus', is encircled by a bandeau extending under the chin.

Body The apron-fronted dress is of white muslin, the skirt ties passing right round the body and forming a bow under the bust, the neckline edged with the frill of a tucker or chemisette. It has short full sleeves, and a skirt with a short train and tucked hem, a fashionable feature of this year. She wears an over-tunic or mantle with a frilled edge (the sleeves may belong to this rather than to the dress).

Accessories The pointed shoes have ribbon ties and very low heels. She wears a necklace and cameo brooch, in the classical style.

4 Thomas, Earl of Haddington, 1802
H. Edridge

Note Fashionable morning and walking dress had now adopted elements of military and country wear, in the form of the riding coat, with its curved fronts, and long boots. Breeches were being replaced by pantaloons, which were tighter fitting and extended to the mid-calf or below. They were usually worn with hessian boots made of patent leather, as developed in the 1790s.

Head The hair is 'a la Titus'.

Body He wears a fine white linen shirt and cravat; double-breasted riding coat; a short waistcoat; and light-coloured breeches or pantaloons.

Accessories He has V-fronted, tasselled hessian boots and short gloves of cotton or leather. Seals hang at the waist.

5 Bella Ibbetson, 1803
J.C. Ibbetson

Note In this period the pelisse was half way between an over-tunic and a coat. Generally long-sleeved and high-waisted, at the beginning of the decade it usually reached just below the knees, but soon extended to the ankles.

Head The small hat of swathed fabric is trimmed with feathers.

Body Her dress is of white muslin, the high-waisted, wrap-over bodice forming a V-neck, edged with a frill. It is worn under a darker pelisse with a shawl collar and wrap-over front, fastening under the bust with a belt. The long tight sleeves have frilled cuffs to match the frilled front edges and hem. The puffed over sleeves caught up at the outer arm are also found on dresses at this date.

Accessories Short gloves and hoop earrings.

6 Self-portrait, 1804
J.C. Ibbetson

Note The artist wears fashionable morning dress. Pantaloons, as shown here, were usually made of light-coloured cloth or cotton, and cut on the bias of the fabric, causing it to stretch and cling to give the closest possible fit. Some were made in fine leather, such as doeskin, which gave a close fit with fewer creases.

Head The top hat is of dark silk or beaver, with a buckled band.

Body He wears a ruffled shirt and black silk stock; a double-breasted morning coat with gilt buttons and high stand-fall collar; and pantaloons.

Accessories Short hessian boots.

7 Miss Ross, 1804
Sir Thomas Lawrence

Head The hair is in classical coils and ringlets.

Body Her day dress is of light silk or cotton muslin with a high-waisted, V-necked bodice and short, puffed sleeves. The skirt of this dress appears to be caught to the bodice at the front and sides, suggesting the popular form of the apron front by which the upper third of the skirt front was slit down the sides, and the flap thus formed was gathered to a drawstring or tape and tied round the waist. The bodice front would fasten separately. Here, the V-neck suggests a wrap-over front, which might lie over or under the top of the skirt. An alternative was for the bodice front to be attached to the skirt flap, and pinned to the shoulders. In both cases buttons, pins or brooches were used as fastenings.

Accessories The pointed shoes are of silk or kid, with very low heels. She has a necklace, brooch and pendant.

8 The Bridges Family, 1804
J. Constable

Note Trousers were fashionable for children
before they were introduced for adults. Both
sexes wore dresses until about four years old.

Head Mrs Bridges has her cropped curls
wound in bandeaux, while the older girls have
long hair combed back in classical coils.

Body All the women wear day dresses of white
muslin with high waists and short, full sleeves,
although the adult version has a more modest
frilled wrap-over front. Father and elder son
both wear frilled shirts with high collars and
white cravats, and dark cloth coats with high
stand-fall collars. The younger boy has a simpler
shirt with frilled collar, a double-breasted tail
coat and high-waisted trousers. The baby
follows adult fashions, but also wears a frilled
muslin cap, threaded with ribbons.

26

9 The Prince of Wales (George IV), 1804
R. Dighton

Note A stylish riding outfit which would have been equally acceptable as fashionable morning or walking dress. Country clothes were high fashion, but only when beautifully tailored in fine quality fabrics. The 'Jean de Bry' riding coat was popular among the Dandies between 1799 and 1808.

Head The hair is 'a la Titus' beneath a top hat of silk or beaver.

Body He wears a shirt with high pointed collar; a wide starched cravat; a 'Jean de Bry' riding coat, distinctive for its high stand-fall collar, almost horizontal lapels, and full gathered shoulders; M-notch collar and gilt buttons; and tight pantaloons.

Accessories He has hessian boots with spurs and wears the Star of the Order of the Garter. The fine leather gloves have decorative points. He carries a rustic-style cane.

10 Robert Southey, 1804
H. Edridge

Note The poet wears informal dress and eschews fashionable extremes. Originally a functional garment worn by sailors, trousers were adopted as informal seaside wear around 1800, and were popularized by the fashionable at Brighton in 1807. At this time, they were usually made of stout buff cotton, and ended well above the ankle. Although looser than pantaloons, they often required a short slit at the hem. They were accepted as general day dress by 1825.

Head The hair is short but avoids the windswept style of high fashion.

Body The shirt collar and cravat are of moderate height. The double-breasted morning coat has a stand-fall collar and M-notch lapels, and he wears matching waistcoat with stand collar. The trousers have a slit at the outside leg.

Accessories Light stockings and lace-up shoes.

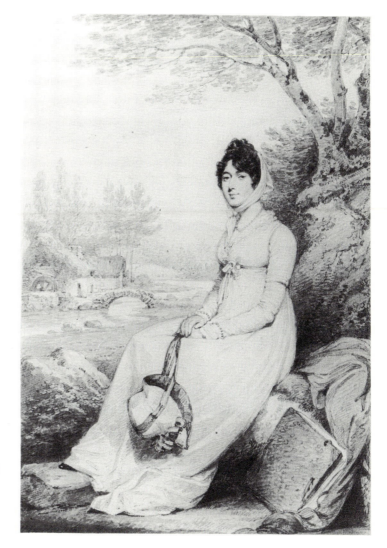

11 Vauxhall Gardens (detail), 1805
Anon. engraving

Note Vauxhall Pleasure Gardens were
frequented by all ranks of society.

Head The women wear their hair trimmed with
jewelled bandeaux, ornamental combs and
feathers.

Body Outfits include several formal afternoon
or evening dresses, similar in style to day
dresses, but with lower necklines and longer
trains. Frilled V-necks are popular, with short
puffed sleeves draped, or caught up and
buttoned on the outer arm. The men's outfits
range from the stylish full evening dress of the
man in the centre, with his crescent-shaped
opera hat, or 'chapeau bras', dark evening coat
and pantaloons and lace-up shoes, to the old
man on the left, who still wears the three-
cornered hat, curled wig, loose frock coat and
breeches with stockings and buckled shoes,
which were last fashionable in the mid-eighteenth
century.

12 Portrait of a young lady, 1806
H. Edridge

Note Supposedly out sketching, she poses in fashionable walking or
morning dress. From 1805 skirts and sleeves were less gathered, and with
the disappearance of trains for day wear after 1806, the silhouette became
straighter and narrower.

Head Her hair is tied in a classical knot of curls under a half
handkerchief.

Body The dress is probably of cotton lawn or muslin, the high-waisted
bodice with a frilled V-neck indicating a wrap-over front. The skirt has an
apron front, shown by the ties passed round the waist and fastened in a
bow at the front. The upper sleeves are short with narrow lower sleeves
extending over the hand (these may be detachable).

Accessories Straw bonnet with ribbon ties and trimmings; low-heeled
pointed shoes; matching necklace and bracelet, probably of coral.

13 Mother and child, 1808
A. Buck

Note An idealized portrait in neo-classical style, but revealing all the basic elements of contemporary fashions.

Head Both adult and child have short, tousled hair.

Body The dresses are of white cotton muslin or lawn. The mother's sleeves are caught up on the outer arm in the style of classical drapery, a common feature in fashionable dresses of 1800-10. The wide, square neckline was common in both day and evening dresses from 1806, and for less formal day dress was worn over a chemisette, which reached to the neck.

Accessories Her shoes are low-cut with very low heels, pointed toes, and decorative ribbon ties. The child's are flat, with high uppers and narrow ribbon laces.

Progress of the Toilet — THE STAYS. Plate 1

14 Progress of the Toilet: the Stays, 1810
J. Gillray

Note Despite the ideal of body-revealing draperies, the fashionable, willowy silhouette of 1810-20 was achieved by hip-length boned stays (Gillray exaggerates the length). To maintain the narrow line, drawers were sometimes preferred to layers of petticoats, but did not become general wear until the 1840s.

Head The fashionable lady being dressed has short hair under a ribbon-trimmed morning cap of fine muslin or lace. The maid wears a cornette.

Body The lady has a short-sleeved chemise with frilled neck, boned stays (into which she inserts a busk), and knee-length drawers. The maid's dress has a fashionably high waistline and long, tight sleeves, but the coloured cotton fabric and ankle-length skirt, and the addition of an apron, are governed by practicality. Her chemisette is normal daytime wear for all classes.

Accessories The lady's silk stockings with decorative clocks and elegant low-cut shoes contrast with the maid's practical lace-ups.

16 Two country women, 1813-18
W.J. White

Note The combination of the loose wrap-over bedgown and simple petticoat (right) was an outfit common to working-class country women from at least the mid-eighteenth century.

Head The old woman on the right wears a silk bonnet with stiffened peak and soft crown, peculiar to the working classes. Her more fashionable companion wears a straw 'cottage' bonnet, with a continuous crown and brim.

Body The old woman's kerchief or small shawl is worn over a long-sleeved, hip-length bedgown, apron and petticoat. Her companion wears a short spencer over a high-waisted dress, in the style fashionable from 1810 to 1815, before the introduction of decorative shoulders and hems.

Accessories The umbrella is a fashionable as well as practical accessory.

15 Portrait of Miss Bathurst, 1812
H. Edridge

Note The pelisse now follows the lines of the dress very closely. Mancherons and tucks introduce a new emphasis on shoulders and hem.

Head The curled hair is combed to the sides of the face with a centre parting, as introduced in 1810. The brimmed hat is trimmed with ribbons.

Body She wears a pelisse which has button fastenings and a belt, a turn-down collar, very long sleeves with mancherons, frogging on the bodice front and tucked hem.

Accessories The low-heeled sandal shoes have ankle ties and three bars across the vamp. She has a knotted neck scarf and long rectangular shawl.

17 Lady Mary Cavendish Bentinck, 1815
J.D. Ingres

Note At the end of the Napoleonic Wars, upper-class visitors to Rome were immortalized by Ingres in a series of souvenir portraits. Stiffened by the frills at the hem, skirts become more angular, while the gathers in the pelisse reveal a new emphasis on the back skirt. Outdoors, gloves and a hat or bonnet would be essential.

Head The hair is in full ringlets on each side of the face.

Body The day dress, with a ruff collar, waist sash and pleated frills at the hem, is worn under a silk pelisse with fur lining, mancherons and cuffs.

Accessories The flat, pointed sandal shoes have ribbon ties and patterned toes (possibly kid with cut-out decorations). She wears a heavy brooch, perhaps a cameo.

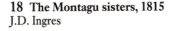

18 The Montagu sisters, 1815
J.D. Ingres

Note Well-to-do young girls (the elder is
thirteen years old) were dressed in a similar style
to adults, except that their sleeves were always
short, shoes more substantial, and they often
wore white cotton trousers or drawers instead of
petticoats. (These became apparent only with the
shorter skirts of the 1820s.) Drawstring necks
were a popular alternative to wrap-over fronts for
adults as well as children.

Head The girls wear low-crowned, wide-
brimmed summer hats of fine straw with ribbon
ties and trimming.

Body Their pelisses, probably of silk, are
thrown open to reveal dresses of light cotton
lawn or muslin, with low drawstring necks, high
waists tied with a sash, and tucks at the hem.

19 Lord Grantham, 1816
J.D. Ingres

Note The gathered shoulders, very long tight
sleeves and high waistline echo those of female
dress. Here, the fall front to the pantaloons is
obvious, as is the crossways pull of the fabric.
Baggy hessians enjoyed a briefly popularity at
this time.

Head He has short, tousled hair with side-
whiskers.

Body He wears a shirt with high pointed collar
swathed in a white starched cravat. The double-
breasted dress coat, with a high stand-fall collar
and M-notch lapels, slightly gathered shoulders,
and flapped pockets at the waist, is worn over a
waistcoat with a stand collar. He has pantaloons.

Accessories He wears hessian boots with
tassels and carries a top hat and short gloves.

20 Sir David Wilkie, 1816
A. Geddes

Note The dressing-gown was a long, loose garment, worn indoors over the shirt, waistcoat and legwear, as an informal alternative to the coat. Although straight-fronted, with an easy shawl collar, this one has a gore in the side to give a flare to the skirt and emphasize the waist, so following a general trend in menswear for a closer fit.

Head He has short, tousled hair.

Body He is dressed in a frilled white shirt and cravat; a dressing-gown of silk or wool damask, patterned with leaves and flowers; and trousers with the legs buttoning at the outer ankle.

Accessories He has light stockings and slippers in the form of flat, heelless mules with a pointed vamp, in the Turkish style.

21 Mr and Mrs Woodhead and the Rev. Comber as a youth, 1816
J.D. Ingres

Head Mrs Woodhead's hair is coiled and held by a comb and bandeau.

Body She wears a spencer, probably of cotton, decorated with bands of ruching caught down with narrow cords, over a dress featuring the very high waist of 1815-20. Both men wear versions of the greatcoat, a form of overcoat fashionable about town and typically long and loose, with straight fronts and buttons to the waist. Woodhead's (left) has a shawl collar, and Comber's a high 'Prussian' collar. When decorated with braid and loop or frog fastenings, like Comber's, they were called 'Polish', 'Hungarian' or 'Russian' coats, and were sometimes fur-lined. Around this date they began to be cut with a close fit and were worn as informal coats with trousers, early versions of the straight-fronted frock coat.

Accessories Mrs Woodhead's neckline is filled in with a handkerchief fastened with a brooch. The dress buttons are almost certainly ornamental. She has a fashionable fringed shawl.

22 Princess Charlotte, 1817
Anon. printed textile

Note This commemorative handkerchief shows the Princess wearing fashionable ball dress. The dominance of white clinging muslins has given way to brightly coloured lightweight silks, which can be puffed and ruched at shoulders and hem, and stiffen a flared skirt. Stripes were particularly fashionable from 1816 to 1820. Indian shawls, with their distinctive pine-cone patterns, were fashionable from the beginning of the century. Copies and variations were produced in France, and in Britain at Norwich and Paisley.

Head The Princess's hair is in a coil, trimmed with a bandeau and flowers.

Body She wears a back-fastening dress, the bodice and puffed sleeves of light silk held by bands of darker silk. The skirt is flared, and the hem decorated with puffs and swags of fabric.

Accessories She has light silk stockings and flat sandal shoes. Her long shawl or 'scarf' is of silk or fine wool, the borders woven with formal flower patterns.

23 The Cloakroom, Clifton Assembly Rooms, 1817
R. Sharples

See colour plate between pp. 96 and 97.

Her Royal Highness,
PRINCESS CHARLOTTE of WALES,
And of SAXE COBURG Saalfeld

Born 7th Jan.y 1796. Died 6th Nov.r 1817.

MONSTROSITIES of 1818

24 Dandies of 1817 Monstrosities of 1818, 1818
G. Cruikshank

Note The Dandies were leaders of male fashion, and excessively clothes-conscious. Both they and their female counterparts demonstrate high fashion at its most extreme. Cruikshank emphasizes the women's larger bonnets, shorter and more decorated hemlines, and the wearing of bustles in the form of semi-circular pads at the back waist.

Head The men's small top hats, or tiny flat hat (an exclusively Dandy style) are in complete contrast to the women's tall-crowned or wide-brimmed bonnets.

Body The men wear excessively high collars and cravats. Their morning coats, or the new straight-fronted frock coat, are cut with high waists, padded chests and gathered shoulders, echoing the high waists and puffed sleeves of the women's pelisses. The men wear either breeches or short wide trousers.

Accessories Footwear is pointed, with top boots and spurs for the men, and flat shoes or sandals for the women. The woman on the right wears a neck chain with watch or scent bottle, and carries a fringed parasol and an embroidered reticule.

25 Mrs James Andrew, 1818
J. Constable

Note Brightly coloured, lustrous silks were softened by being overlaid with soft nets or 'aerophanes'. As the wearer moved, a shimmering effect was produced in the skirt and sleeves, highlighted by the silk trimmings on bodice, sleeves and hem.

Head She wears her hair with a centre parting and side curls, under a full-crowned cap of fine lawn or muslin, tied under the chin, and trimmed with flowers and ribbons.

Body She is dressed in a high-waisted dress of silk gauze or net, with an under-dress of plain silk or satin. Bust and shoulders are emphasized by applied bands of silk. The long, full sleeves are frilled at the wrist.

Accessories There is a silk sash at the waist and, beneath the dress, a chemisette with a frilled neck. Her other accessories are neckchains, a brooch and rings.

26 The Duke of Argyll, 1819
R. Dighton

Note The Duke is dressed in fashionable outdoor wear. Early frock coats are still very similar to greatcoats, although perhaps more fitted, since they are no longer top coats. This one is in the latest style, with its roll collar, straight fronts, buttons down to the waist, long tight sleeves with cuffs, and a back vent with side pleats. It features the longer waist which appeared from about 1818. This gave a closer fit which soon required a dart or seam at the waist, although these were not general until 1823.

Head He has a top hat.

Body His shirt has a high pointed collar, swathed in a cravat. The striped waistcoat has a stand collar. He wears an early form of the frock coat and trousers.

Accessories Boots and gloves.

**27 Lady Catherine
Manners, 1819-20**
Sir William Beechey

Note She is dressed
in fashionable full
evening dress. Most
fashionable skirts of
this date had their
hems decorated and
stiffened with
flounces, rouleaux, or
other applied
trimmings. The plain
flowing lines of this
one may be influenced
by the painter's
preference for flowing
draperies.

Head Her centrally
parted hair with side
curls and back ringlets
is worn under a silk
turban trimmed with
pearls and feathers.

Body The high-
waisted silk dress has
a low neck edged with
a lace frill or tucker,
short puffed sleeves
caught up by bands of
darker silk and a skirt
with a train.

Accessories As well
as a lace 'scarf' shawl
she has pearl drop
earrings, a neck chain
with pendant or scent
bottle, chain bracelets
and a rectangular
brooch.

28 Court dress, 1820
Engraving from *Ackermann's Repository of Arts*

Note The fashion plate ideal of court dress.
The elaborate costumes worn for official
occasions at the royal court were governed by
strict regulations, and were slow to reflect
changes in fashion. An ostrich feather headdress,
long gloves and a train were essential
requirements, and the components of robe and
separate stomacher, bodice and petticoat, were
based on eighteenth-century styles. It was only
with the accession of George IV in 1820 that the
eighteenth-century hoop was finally discarded.
Here the narrow skirt, short puffed sleeves and
relatively high waist are the main concessions to
current fashions.

Head The ostrich plume headdress has a pearl
bandeau and lace lappets.

Body Her short-sleeved, trained robe of silk is
trimmed with lace and pearls, and the silk
bodice, with stomacher-style front, is
ornamented with pearls. A separate satin petticoat
trimmed with silver and artificial roses is worn beneath a
shorter lace petticoat.

Accessories She has white kid gloves, white
satin shoes, pearl necklace and earrings and an
embroidered silk fan.

29 Tom and Jerry at the Royal Academy (detail), 1821
I.R. and G. Cruikshank

Note Fashionable day dress is shown in this scene.

Head Women's headwear includes (from the left) a feathered turban, a high-crowned hat and a range of wide-brimmed bonnets trimmed with ostrich plumes and a veil.

Body Women's pelisses are still very high-waisted, with mancherons and braid trimming. Hem lengths vary, but puffs and vandyking are a feature. On the left is a riding habit, trimmed with military-style braid. The men wear morning coats or (at the back) a frock coat, while the parson (right) wears clerical dress. Greatcoats feature cape collars (back view right). Breeches still compete with straight trousers of varying lengths, including (centre) voluminous 'Cossacks', pleated to the waist and gathered to the ankle, a style inspired by the Czar's visit to London in 1814.

Accessories Women carry reticules of fabric or leather.

30 Tom and Jerry in the Saloon at Covent Garden (detail), 1821
I.R. and G. Cruikshank

Note The men generally wear day dress, but many of the women are in full evening dress.

Head Evening headdresses for women include curled hair in a knot, with combs and feathers, or feathered turbans.

Body Evening dresses have low décolletage with puffed sleeves and padded hems. Day dress necklines are modestly filled in with a chemisette, while the woman in the riding habit (left) demonstrates the fashionable obsession informality and the popularity of riding dress for all occasions. The men generally wear morning coats and knee breeches or pantaloons. An exception (right) is the frock coat with military-style frogging, and trousers with instep straps to keep them taut (popular from 1817).

31 Walking dress, 1821
Engraving from *Ackermann's Repository of Arts*

Note This fashionable ideal has the slightly dropped waistline, puffed shoulders and padded decorations at the hem.

Head She has centrally-parted hair with side curls. The watered silk bonnet has a slightly turned-up brim lined with tufted gauze and tied with silk ribbons. According to the fashion-plate description, the crown is trimmed with silk leaves, plaited straw, and flowers.

Body A ruff with double frill is attached to the chemisette. The silk spencer, with its V-shaped satin panel, small falling collar, shoulder puffs and tight sleeves are all edged with frills and bands of satin. Beneath is a dress of cotton muslin, the hem trimmed with a rouleau, puffs of muslin, and a pleated flounce.

Accessories Black kid shoes.

32 Hannah More, 1822
H.W. Pickersgill

Note This elderly playwright and reformer wears a simple day dress which, with its very high waistline and smooth, ungathered shoulders, is in the fashionable style of 1815-20.

Head The centrally-parted hair is slightly curled at the sides. The high-crowned, frilled muslin cap ties under the chin, and is trimmed with silk ribbons.

Body She wears a silk dress with high waist, the V-neck filled in by a chemisette with a ruff collar. The sleeves have muslin frills at the wrist.

Accessories A scarf shawl of silk or fine wool, with fashionably patterned borders and ends is draped over her shoulders. She holds a scent bottle.

33 The Countryside in May (detail), 1822-4
Anon. engraving

Note City fashions were copied in the country, but were usually less extreme and were modified according to the wearer's occupation.

Head The woman on the right wears a fashionable 'Marie Stuart' bonnet, while the barmaid has a simple high-crowned day cap.

Body and Accessories The more fashionable woman wears a pelisse with concealed front fastening, frilled collar, puffed shoulders and frilled hem. The barmaid's dress has fashionably puffed shoulders, but the neckline is covered with an old-fashioned handkerchief, crossed at the front. This is tucked into the bib of her barmaid's apron, which is pinned to her bodice. The country man wears the long, flap-pocketed greatcoat. Its loose fit is unfashionable, as are his large neckcloth, which he wears instead of a cravat, and his top boots. The girl has the hat, low neckline and short sleeves common to children's fashions.

34 Lord Byron, 1823
Count D'Orsay

Note Newly recovered from an illness, his fashionable day clothes hang rather loose upon him. In this decade the clothes of both sexes featured fuller shoulders and a narrower waistline.

Head His hair is short and tousled.

Body His shirt is finely gathered to a high, pointed collar and he wears a black silk stock and a morning coat with a roll collar cut high at the back and M-notch lapels. The cut-away fronts are now squared off, and the tails broad and square. The shoulders are gathered and the sleeves long and tight. The waistcoat is cut in the latest fashion with a slightly pointed waist. The trousers have instep straps.

Accessories He is probably wearing light-coloured gaiters over square-toed boots. There is a decorative, perhaps jewelled, pin fastening the shirt front. He carries a cane with plain short handle, less showy than those with strings and tassels.

45

35 Woman in day dress, 1824-7
'Mansion'

Note Between 1822 and 1827 the waistline drops to its natural level, sleeves widen, and with 'Marie Stuart' caps and ruffs, the look is self-conciously Elizabethan.

Head Fashionably parted hair with side curls and a knot on the crown is worn under a 'Marie Stuart' morning cap of fine muslin, the double frill edged with lace, and silk ribbon ties under the chin.

Body A matching neck ruff is attached to a chemisette and she has a bow of striped silk gauze ribbon. Her dress is of fine lawn or muslin, the fan-shaped gathers emphasizing shoulders and waist. The straight edge of the cotton lining is visible level with the shoulder. The sleeves are gathered at the shoulder over short puffed undersleeves. The flared skirt is gathered to the bodice at the sides and back (probably over a small bustle pad).

Accessories Watered silk belt with metal buckle.

36 Beauties of Brighton, 1825
A. 'Crowquill'

Note Under the Prince Regent Brighton became a centre of fashion frequented by Dandies.

Head The Dandies wear top hats, the women fashionable wide-brimmed hats. The man in the centre has the newly fashionable long side-whiskers which merge with his lady-friend's curls.

Body The men's high-pointed shirt collars and cravats are worn with tight morning coats (left), open to reveal waistcoats with shawl collars and pointed waists. Tight pantaloons and patterned stockings (left) are still an alternative to trousers with instep straps (centre). Tight-waisted coats (centre) echo women's pelisses, now cut with huge gigot sleeves and ever wider gored skirts with decorated hems.

37 The Rev. Ryland, 1827
D. Maclise

Note This is fashionable day dress for men. In the 1820s men's coats reflect women's fashions with their gigot sleeves, dropped waistline and tight fit. Some Dandies wore chest padding and stays to achieve the fashionable hour-glass silhouette.

Head His short hair is still worn brushed forward rather than back, as was usual in this decade.

Body He wears a high, pointed shirt collar with cravat; a high-cut waistcoat; a morning coat with roll collar cut very high at the back, M-notch lapels, long, narrow sleeves, gathered at the shoulder and extending over the hand; and light trousers.

Accessories Watch or seals attached to the waist.

47

39 Woman in dinner dress, 1830
F. Cruikshank

Note Although painted in 1830, the sitter's dress is in the style fashionable in the late 1820s. Berets were popular evening wear throughout the 1820s and early 1830s, and were usually worn at an angle after 1827. Cut steel and chased gold were used for buckles as for other jewellery.

Head Centrally-parted hair with sausage-shaped side curls and a knot on the crown is worn under a silk or velvet beret, trimmed with ribbons and feathers.

Body The silk dress features a vandyked neck and cuffs and a horizontal neckline emphasizing full gigot sleeves. The skirt has a deep flounced hem headed by a twisted rouleau.

Accessories She wears a silk belt with ornate metal buckle, silk shoes with square toes, a short necklace and rings. Her glove, probably of kid, is fashionably short, but plain (many had frilled or scalloped wrists).

38 'Nothing extenuate nor aught set down in malice', 1827
Anon. engraving

Note From 1825 hats, sleeves and skirts grew steadily wider. Down-filled sleeve puffs padded the shoulders, heavy corded and flounced cotton petticoats stiffened the skirt, tight, boned stays narrowed the waist, and a bustle made of cotton flounces gave fullness to the back of the skirt. This caricature exaggerates the shape for 1827, but by 1830 this was almost a reality.

Head The wide-brimmed hat has a wide ribbon tie left hanging loose. The trimmings are bows, leaves and sprigs of feathers or grass. She has centrally-parted hair with sausage-shaped side curls and a knot on the crown.

Body The dress consists of a draped bodice, narrow waist (now at natural level), large gigot sleeves and a wide skirt, gathered at sides and back, with a flounced hem.

Accessories Her accessories include a ribbon bow and sash, long drop earrings, short kid gloves with vandyked wrists, square-toed sandal shoes and an embroidered handkerchief.

40 An Irresistible Arming for Conquest, 1828-30
Anon. engraving

Note A fashionable woman in her underwear, being dressed for the evening. Stays and bustles were essential to achieve the hour-glass shape fashionable from 1825 to 1835.

Head The hair, in a high chignon (a variant on the Apollo knot) with curls and ringlets, is decorated with an ornamental comb and ostrich plumes. The maid has a be-ribboned cotton day cap.

Body The lady wears tightly laced boned stays over a sleeveless chemise, and a bustle of cotton flounces tying round the waist. The maid's dress, although plain, features a fashionably fitted waist, full skirt and gigot sleeves.

Accessories The mistress has the white silk stockings, square-toed black satin sandal shoes, drop earrings and short necklace fashionable with formal dress.

41 Mrs Ellen Sharples, 1829-31
R. Sharples

Note The artist's mother in fashionable day dress. Still wider gigot sleeves are emphasized by wide caps, pelerines and capes. Within a year or two, bodice pleats will converge well above the waist, adding another almost horizontal line.

Head The hair in side curls and a knot is hidden by a cap of pleated, stiffened blonde lace.

Body Her neckline is filled by a handkerchief and she wears a double pelerine of blonde lace. The silk dress has a bodice decorated with flat pleats converging at the waist and padded gigot sleeves. The cloak, apparently of figured or brocaded silk, has a plain lining and an attached cape.

Accessories Brooch and armlet, probably set with a cameo, mosaic, or semi-precious stone.

50

42 Queen Adelaide, 1831
Sir William Beechey

Note The Queen poses in evening dress. Blonde lace, with its distinctive sheen of silk, was fashionable for veils, trimmings etc. throughout the 1820s and 1830s.

Head The Queen's hair is dressed in a chignon formed from stiffened loops of hair (a variant on the Apollo knot), with sausage-shaped side curls. She has a pearl bandeau and veil.

Body The muslin tucker is edged with a lace ruff and the dress, apparently of velvet, has a wide neck trimmed with a vandyked frill extending over the shoulders. The large gigot oversleeves are of blonde lace. The waist is emphasized with a belt. Her skirt is set flat to the waist at the front (clearly not the full pleated dome-shape of the current fashion plates).

Accessories She wears drop earrings, matching pendant brooch, and a gold watch and chain. A bouquet and a handkerchief were both popular evening accessories.

44 Mrs Thomas Hood, 1832-4
Anon.

Note She is wearing evening or dinner dress, with the addition of a pelerine. Sleeves were at their fullest between 1830 and 1833, with pelerines emphasizing the width.

Head The hair is centrally-parted with a knot on the crown and side curls. Her hat probably consists of wired puffs of brocaded or embroidered silk, edged with a fringe (a similar type in a fashion plate of 1827 was called a 'Vienna toque').

Body The double pelerine is probably of embroidered white muslin. It appears to extend at the front, and may be a fichu-pelerine, with its two ends tucked into the belt. The dress has decorative lapels resting on large gigot sleeves, a wide belt and a skirt pleated to the waist.

Accessories These include drop earrings, brooch and neck chain, probably with a watch, eyeglass, or scent bottle tucked into the belt.

43 Benjamin Disraeli, 1833
After D. Maclise

Note Young Disraeli's style of morning dress reflects his Dandified tastes. In this decade, lavish tastes found expression in colourful patterned waistcoats and a variety of jewellery, including studs, pins, rings etc.

Head The hair is fashionably mid-length with a side parting.

Body The shirt has frilled front and cuffs and the wide cravat is tied in the 'waterfall' style, with a decorative pin (he favoured white satin cravats). His shawl-collared waistcoat is very tight. Fitted, and possibly padded, the morning coat has a roll collar and lapels cut high at the back, M-notch lapels, and very long sleeves, worn open to reveal cravat and waistcoat. His trousers have instep straps.

Accessories His footwear consists of square-toed pumps with ribbon bows and he has a watch and chain tucked into the waistcoat watch pocket.

45 Interior of the Gallery of Watercolour Artists (detail), 1834
G. Scharf

Note The middle-class visitors to the gallery are in outdoor dress.

Head The women wear bonnets with deep oval brims hiding the sides of the face, and bavolets. Fashionable trimmings are ribbon bows and feathers, and broad ribbon ties under the chin (lace veils to shade the face, or hang down one side from the brim, were also popular).

Body Broad white muslin pelerines are worn or (right) a fichu-pelerine. Pelisses have large gigot sleeves. The men demonstrate the popularity of frock coats and trousers.

Accessories The seated woman has an umbrella (as opposed to the smaller parasol), and the one on the right wears a neck chain, probably suspending a watch, scent bottle, or eyeglass. She carries an embroidered reticule.

47 A young girl, 1834
T.M. Joy

Note Day dress for young girls was a simplified form of adult evening dress, with the addition of long drawers. Around the middle of the decade, neater hairstyles, with the hair drawn back at the sides in a loop or plait, were replacing elaborate knots and side curls.

Head The girl's hair is plaited at the sides and arranged in a knot on the crown.

Body The dress has a low décolletage, beret sleeves, and waist sash. The skirt is gathered with a deep hem. She wears frilled drawers of white linen or cotton.

Accessories Silk or cotton stockings and square-toed sandal shoes, probably of black satin. She has neck chains and a pendant.

46 A woman in evening dress, 1834
Watt after A.E. Chalon

Note A fairly plain evening outfit, perhaps simplified by the artist. Popular accessories would have included flowers in the hair, long pendant earrings, short necklace, elbow-length white kid gloves with frilled tops, and a small fan or bouquet of flowers.

Head Centrally parted hair with side curls is arranged in stiffened loops on the crown, a version of the Apollo knot.

Body The silk evening dress has a low décolletage trimmed at the back and sides with a standing collar, probably of stiffened blonde lace. The bodice is draped *à la Sevigné*, in horizontal folds divided by a boned band. Beret sleeves are trimmed with bows. The waistline is round, and she wears a belt. (From 1832 some evening bodices were slightly pointed at the front and back waist.) The full skirt is pleated to the bodice.

48 Florence Nightingale and her sister, 1836-7
W. White

Note These are middle-class girls in informal morning dress. From 1836 shoulder lines dropped-sleeves began to deflate, and hemlines fell from the ankle to the instep. Mittens were fashionable for day and evening in the 1830s and 1840s.

Head Both women have centrally-parted hair smoothed into a plaited knot on the crown.

Body They are wearing white muslin pelerines and day dresses with simple draped bodice and belted waist. The smooth, dropped shoulder line leads to versions of the full gigot sleeves: (right) the 'Imbecile', full to the cuff, and (left) the 'Donna Maria', full to the elbow, and then tight to the wrist. Their skirts are full and gathered.

Accessories The sister on the left has square-toed shoes, short mittens of black net or lace and a linen or cotton apron.

49 Queen Victoria, 1837–8
A.E. Chalon

Note The young Queen is seen here in ordinary day dress. Embroidered aprons were fashionable 'at home' wear, proclaiming domesticity, although too ornate to be practical.

Head Her hair is looped over the ears into a knot at the back.

Body She wears a deep-caped lace pelerine and a dress of watered silk with dropped shoulders, with a type of 'Victoria' sleeve, full in the middle below a pleated mancheron. There is a buckled waist belt above the full pleated skirt.

Accessories Her shoes are flat and square-toed. Other accessories are neck chains, a brooch, bracelets and an embroidered black satin apron. On the ground is a silk bonnet trimmed with a bird of paradise, the brim lined with ruched tulle or lace.

50 The Duchess of Kent, 1837–8
A.E. Chalon

Note Queen Victoria's mother in fashionable outdoor dress.

Head The hair is plaited over the ears, with a knot at the back, and a velvet band across the brow. She wears an oval-brimmed bonnet with mentonnières and lining of ruched net or lace and flowers, the crown trimmed with ribbons and a bird of paradise.

Body The double collar is of net or lace. She wears a watered silk pelisse dress, with cross-over draped bodice; sleeves with multiple bouffants, a belt with ornate metal buckle; and a skirt trimmed with lace frills *en tablier*.

Accessories She has short gloves and squared-toed shoes. Hanging from her neck chain is a watch or scent bottle tucked into the belt. Her bracelets include a fashionable matching pair of bands.

51 Mrs Harris Prendergast, 1838
A. Geddes

Note This is fashionable evening dress at a time when fashion favoured a revival of mid-seventeenth-century styles including ringlets, lace berthas, and bows on shoulders and gloves. The draperies emphasize width, while the curved bertha creates the popular drooping shoulder line.

Head Her hair is drawn into a plaited knot, with a plaited band and ringlets.

Body The satin dress has a heart-shaped décolletage, horizontal drapes across shoulder and bust, and obvious vertical boning. The short sleeves are trimmed with ribbon bows, falling loosely at the elbow. The curved bertha of blonde lace falls low over the outer arms, giving the effect of a ruffled oversleeve. She wears a full, pleated skirt.

Accessories On her right arm she wears an evening glove, probably of kid, edged with ribbon bows (she holds the other). Other accessories are a neck chain, a pearl bracelet with cameo clasp, and rings.

52 Youth and Age, 1839
J.C. Horsley

Head and Body The old country labourer wears the soft, wide-brimmed 'bullycock' hat and linen smock – characteristic country wear of the late eighteenth and most of the nineteenth centuries. These smocks, in white, brown or blue, were often elaborately embroidered in the same colour, on chest, shoulders and wrists. He wears cord or leather breeches. The little girl's bonnet, pelisse and drawstring reticule imitate adult fashions, but her ankle-strap shoes with ribbon bows are typical child's wear.

Accessories Gaiters and sturdy leather boots were worn by country labourers long after trousers had become fashionable.

53 Princess Victoire, 1839
Sir Edwin Landseer

Note The Princess is wearing formal summer day or evening dress. As the knot of the hair drops to the back of the head, the shoulder line slopes, and the sleeve fullness drops to the elbow and below, the whole silhouette deflates, introducing the elongated, angular shape of the 1840s.

Head Her long hair is drawn from a centre parting into a plaited knot at the back, and into side ringlets which Landseer wittily compares with the spaniel's ears.

Body The dress of sprigged muslin has a low décolletage edged with a deep lace bertha. Victoria sleeves are trimmed with bows. The gathered skirt has a flounced hem.

Accessories She carries a lace-edged handkerchief. On the balustrade is a parasol of silk or lace, with a tasselled cord.

54 Mrs Edward Elliot in evening dress, 1839-40
After A.E. Chalon

Note This is very similar to the evening dress worn by Mrs Harris Prendergast in 1838 (fig. 51), but the pointed waist is now essential. Concurrent with a revival of seventeenth-century motifs is the popularity for evening wear of silks brocaded with flowers in eighteenth-century style. Many eighteenth-century dresses were altered for re-use between 1835 and 1845.

Head Her hair is arranged in a knot at the back and in ringlets, although the very loose flowing ringlets may be artistic licence.

Body The evening dress is of figured or brocaded silk, the wide décolletage trimmed with a lace bertha and ribbon bows. It has a pointed waistline, with obvious boning. Loose draped and ruffled sleeves are caught up with a bow. The dress has a full, pleated skirt.

Accessories Her mittens are probably of embroidered net. She wears a bracelet with fashionable heart-shaped locket and holds a lace-edged handkerchief.

55 Lady Elizabeth Villiers, 1841-3
After A.E. Chalon

Note She is wearing fashionable day dress. Although the fullness is still centred on the back, skirts are becoming wider. From 1841 they contain more material which is gauged to the waist, a technique whereby the fabric is finely gathered and attached by alternate pleats. This produces a characteristic dome-shaped skirt. Here, the width is emphasized by the horizontal bands of trimming.

Head Her long hair is arranged in a knot and ringlets.

Body The dress of watered silk is trimmed with bands of velvet and black lace flounces, giving the effect of a bertha on the bodice. The long, tight sleeves have a band of trimmings as the only remnant of the bouffants of 1837-40. The skirt is full and gathered.

Accessories She carries the ubiquitous lace-edged handkerchief.

56 Unknown woman, 1842
W. Buckler

Note Another example of fashionable day dress
of the early 1840s.

Head The hair is draped over the ears into a
knot at the back (a neater alternative to ringlets,
popular for daytime).

Body A lace pelerine is trimmed with rosettes.
The dress of silk, figured or brocaded with a
trailing stem pattern has a pointed waist, with
obvious boning, long, tight sleeves and a full,
gathered skirt.

Accessories A long scarf shawl was a popular
summer wrap and this one features the traditional
cone pattern of embroidered Kashmir shawls.
This may be an Indian import, or one of the
many woven imitations made in France, or in
Britain, in centres like Paisley (whose name
became synonymous with the pattern). The flat,
square-toed shoes are probably of black satin. A
lace-edged handkerchief and bouquet were both
fashionable accessories. Her bonnet is in the
almost tubular shape typical of 1838-50,
trimmed with silk ribbons and ostrich plumes.

57 Unknown gentleman, 1842
W. Huggins

Note Fashionable day dress is shown here.
Gathered sleeves and chest padding are
reduced, waists lengthen, and waistcoats are cut
with a pointed front, all features which echo
changes in women's fashions, and which
produce a more streamlined silhouette. His
trousers feature a fall front, although the fly
fastening, first used around 1823, became
general in the 1840s.

Head He has smoothed hair with a side parting
(many wore it longer and curled under at the
back).

Body He wears a high shirt collar with a large
silk cravat or 'scarf', covering the shirt. The
double-breasted frock coat has a velvet collar,
narrow sleeves and cuffs. The waistcoat, of
embroidered or brocaded silk, has a wide roll
collar and lapels, and pointed waist. The narrow
trousers probably have instep straps.

Accessories Chained cravat pin, watch chain
and ring.

58 Two Dandies, 1843
A. 'Crowquill'

Note As the male silhouette becomes more streamlined, flamboyance is expressed in brightly patterned neckwear, waistcoats and trousers. Paletots had many versions. These may be (left) the short pea- or monkey-jacket, and (right) the pilot coat, noted for its large buttons and slanted pockets.

Head They have long hair and flat-brimmed top hats.

Body They wear high shirt collars with (left) a brightly patterned silk cravat tied in a bow, and (right) a scarf cravat. Their paletots have fashionable turn-down collars, and horizontal slit or flapped pockets. The narrow trousers have gaiter bottoms. By contrast, the shopkeeper is unfashionable with his short hair, frilled shirt front and baggy trousers.

Accessories Footwear consists of narrow, square-toed shoes. They wear short gloves and carry thin canes, probably of ebony or bamboo, with gold knobs and tassels.

59 The Royal Railroad Carriage (detail), 1843
Anon. engraving

Note Prince Albert and Queen Victoria with their children and attendants in fashionable day dress.

Head The women wear tubular bonnets with dipped sides, decorated with ostrich feathers and bonnet veil.

Body All the women wear lace-trimmed pelerines and dresses with pointed waists (the Queen's being the longest and most fashionable). The attendants have slightly less fashionable Victoria sleeves. The Queen wears a mantle with armhole slits. Prince Albert wears a scarf cravat, probably a frock coat, and trousers apparently with gaiter bottoms. His fashionably sloping shoulders, pointed waist and small feet echo female styles. The infant Prince of Wales (right) in his plumed hat, is still young enough to wear a dress like his sister's. The baby wears a cap and formal long lace carrying robe.

61 Lady Ruthven, 1843-8
Photograph by Hill and Adamson

Note Summer outdoor clothes are shown here. The skirt of the 1840s is long enough to hide the feet and form a slight train.

Head The tubular bonnet has dipping sides, a brim which appears to be openwork straw plaits, a crown covered with fabric and simple ribbon trimmings. Her short bavolet juts out at the back as she looks downwards.

Body She has a white muslin collar. The folded square shawl is of black net (both hand-made and machined net were worn). The frilled edging is probably embroidered net rather than bobbin lace. The day dress is of striped silk or one of the popular mixed fabrics of silk and wool, or wool and cotton. The fitted, boned bodice puckers where it fastens down the back. Long tight sleeves fit below a line of dark piping at the shoulder.

60 Sisters,1842-6
J. Sant

Head Both girls have centrally-parted hair with ringlets. The elder has a knot and single ringlets.

Body The elder wears a satin day dress with a lace collar, long, tight sleeves and frilled cotton undersleeves. The sloping shoulders, long pointed waist, dome-shaped skirt and plain, clean-cut outlines are typical of the 1840s. Pleats, folds (and perhaps piped seams) are the only trimmings. Converging to the waist, and set *en tablier* on the skirt, they serve to emphasize the main structure. The younger girl's muslin dress, trimmed with ribbon and lace, has the low neckline, short sleeves and calf-length skirt of childhood, although the deep bertha and long pointed waist imitate adult styles. She has frilled cotton drawers (which were beginning to be worn by adults).

Accessories They both wear flat, square-toed shoes with ribbon ties.

62 The Bromley family, 1844
F.M. Brown

Head and Body The three women on the right follow the fashions, with centrally-parted hair draped over the ears into a knot, deep lace berthas, formal day dresses with low necks and very long, pointed waists. Two have narrow sleeves with lace cuffs, the third the new bell-shaped sleeve worn over separate white cotton undersleeves or *engageantes*. The woman on the left still retains the sausage-shaped side curls, long earrings, and wide frilled lace cap of the mid-1830s. (The fashionable cap, when worn, would have been flat and close-fitting, with lappets hanging over the ears.) Her round-necked dress with sleeves puffed below the elbow is equally unfashionable.

Accessories The bouquets, in holders of metal or cut paper, are popular accessories with formal dress.

Note For dresses of fashionable cut, the skirts
are surprisingly narrow, showing little evidence
of the usual layers of stiffened petticoats. Bare
arms, without undersleeves, would be
unacceptable for an older woman. Flounced
skirts become more popular after 1843.

Head Both have hair looped over the ears into a
knot.

Body The sister on the left wears a day dress,
probably of cotton, printed with fashionable
stripes. The bodice is draped to emphasize the
long, pointed waist, finished with a sash and
rosette. The skirt is flounced.

Accessories Sideways on the table is her
bonnet, the brim lined with pleated fabric. Her
sister wears a dark mantle or shawl, and carries a
straw bonnet trimmed inside with flowers.

63 Mrs Barker, 1844
Photograph by Hill and Adamson

Head Her hair is looped over the ears into a knot.

Body The collar of white muslin has whitework embroidery. Her day
dress, probably of cotton or a light wool mixture is printed with fashionable
stripes and has a long pointed waist; the material is cut on the cross, with a
centre front seam, so that the stripes echo the line of the waist. Separate
panels are draped in folds at the front. Long tight sleeves are also cut on
the cross to give a close fit, with decorative folds. Narrow undersleeves
probably match the collar. The skirt is gauged to the bodice, allowing
maximum material in the ever-widening skirt.

Accessories She wears a plaid shawl and has a long neck chain, probably
suspending a gold watch.

66 Baroness Burdett-Coutts, 1847-50
W.C. Ross

Note The evening dresses of this decade were restrained in style, characterized by the contrast of plain silk and rich lace. This is probably expensive hand-made bobbin lace, but the cheaper machined laces were stylish and popular. The fashion plate ideal would have a wider skirt, and flowers in the hair.

Head Her hair is looped back in a plaited knot.

Body The silk dress has a décolletage edged with a tucker and a flounced lace bertha, sleeves with lace ruffles and a flounced skirt.

Accessories She wears a lace shawl, neck ribbon with pendant and bracelets, including two of black velvet ribbon with a decorative clasp or locket.

65 Mrs Bell, 1843-8
Photograph by Hill and Adamson

Note The self-conscious mediaevalism of the 1840s was reflected in dress as in other art forms.

Head She has centrally-parted hair with plaited knot, comb and ringlets.

Body Her day dress is of silk, figured or damasked with stylized scrolling leaves, recalling mediaeval designs and has trimmings of tucks, velvet ribbon and black lace. The neck is edged with a frill of muslin or lace. The bodice has a cape-like front panel, emphasizing the sloping shoulders, low-set sleeves, and long, pointed waist. A trimming of ornamental, thread-covered toggles and beads runs down the centre front (a precursor of the front-buttoning jacket bodice of the 1850s). The long, tight sleeves have braid trimming at the cuffs.

Accessories Her neck chain has a watch and key or seal. She wears a brooch of delicate intertwined flowers and stems, with pendant flower, in the Romantic style.

67 The County Hunt Ball (detail), 1850
Anon. engraving

Note The provincial middle and upper middle
classes here wear full evening dress.

Head The women usually wear their hair
looped into a plaited knot, trimmed with flowers
or feathers (although ringlets are still worn).

Body The short-sleeved silk ball dresses have
the décolletage edged with a lace bertha

decorated with ribbons and flowers, long pointed
waists and full skirts, often trimmed with lace
flounces, or plain but open at the front to reveal
a flounced underskirt. The men wear black or
white ties. Evening tail coats were cut long in the
waist until 1855. The single-breasted, shawl-
collared waistcoats are usually black or white.
Narrow trousers are now generally without
straps.

Accessories Men's evening pumps were often
buckled.

68 Answering the Emigrant's Letter, 1850
J. Collinson

Note A country labourer and his family.

Head The wife wears her hair smoothed into a knot, under a simple
gathered cotton day cap of the type worn by the fashionable classes only in
the morning.

Body Her short-sleeved dress of linen, cotton or wool, reveals
unfashionably bare arms, and lacks the boned bodice and stiffened
petticoats essential to the fashionable silhouette. Her linen apron is purely
functional. The husband wears a neck scarf. His linen shirt has the square-
cut body, shoulder band, and full sleeves common to all classes for most of
the century (the chief variable was the quality of the material). His short
waistcoat and breeches are old-fashioned. The seated boy wears a plain
country smock.

Accessories Both males have coarse stockings and sturdy leather boots.

69 Bloomerism, an American Custom, 1851
J. Leech

Note Around 1850, Mrs Bloomer, an American reformer, demanded that
women be allowed to wear trousers instead of the burdensome long skirts
and layers of heavy petticoats. She promoted a 'Bloomer' costume,
consisting of wide-brimmed hat, loose, knee-length tunic and ankle-length
baggy trousers, not unlike children's outfits of the period. Although worn
by a number of Americans, it appears to have been too advanced for
Britain. However, Englishwomen had worn neck ties with day dresses
throughout the 1840s, a basqued jacket bodice had become acceptable by
1851, and wide-brimmed hats were being introduced for informal wear.

Head and Body The conservative Englishwoman (right) wears an oval-
brimmed bonnet, wide-sleeved mantle, and long, dome-shaped skirt. The
Americans (left) wear Leech's version of 'Bloomer' costume, consisting of
a wide hat, neck tie, basqued jacket bodice, flounced skirt and baggy
trousers.

70 The Awakening Conscience, 1853
W.H. Hunt

Note A fallen woman and her lover, in a rare depiction of women's informal undress.

Head The man has fashionably short hair and full side whiskers (a centre parting was the mode with elegant young men).

Body He wears a dashing scarf neckcloth, velvet coat, and contrasting trousers with decorative banding. The woman wears a striped cotton dressing jacket trimmed with lace and a silk ribbon bow, the sleeves of fashionable pagoda shape. Probably to add colour and drapery, the artist has swathed her hips in a fashionable shawl, whose borders are woven or embroidered with Indian cone patterns. Her waist-length cotton petticoat is trimmed with tucks and *broderie anglaise*.

Accessories Her square-toed shoes probably have the newly fashionable one-inch heels. His ankle boots have side buttons, or, more probably, elastic sides and decorative buttons. Elastic-sided boots were patented in 1837.

71 The Last of England, 1852-5
F.M. Brown

Note Middle-class emigrants to Australia, dressed for the long sea voyage.

Head The man wears an informal, wide-brimmed, beaver or wool felt hat, called a 'wideawake' ('because of having no nap', *Punch*, 1849), secured to his coat button by a cord. His wife's hair is fashionably draped over her ears into a knot at the back, with a plaited braid across the top of the head. This was a popular feature, typical of the fuller, rounder hairstyles of this decade. Her bonnet has the flared, elliptical brim of the early 1850s, revealing a trimming of puffed ribbon. A bonnet veil blows out over the umbrella.

Body The man wears a double-breasted heavy wool greatcoat, with checked lining; his wife a simple, non-fashionable, fringed shawl of finely checked wool, pinned together under the chin, over a plain day dress.

Accessories She has short leather gloves.

73 Ramsgate Sands (detail), 1854
After W.P. Frith

Note Apart from actual swimming costumes, no special clothing was worn at the seaside. The suntan was the mark of the country labourer, and so was consciously avoided by the fashionable.

Head The woman on the right wears a straw bonnet with flared brim, lined with ruched fabric, typical of the early 1850s. Her companion's ringlets are now more usually worn by young women, or restricted to evening dress. She has a silk bonnet, and both she and the child wear an ugly to protect them from the sun.

Body An alternative to the shawl (right) is the frilled silk mantle (left). The woman on the left has lifted the skirt of her day dress, revealing her white cotton petticoats trimmed with coarse lace or openwork embroidery.

72 Queen Victoria and Prince Albert, 1854
Photograph by R. Fenton

Note The royal couple in fashionable day dress. Transparent muslins, warp-printing, frills, flounces and trimmings all combine to create the characteristic blurred silhouette of women's dress in the 1850s.

Head The Queen's hair is draped over her ears into a knot at the back of the head. Her elaborate cap of frilled muslin, lace and ribbons, with hanging streamers, is worn on the back of the head, like fashionable bonnets.

Body Her dress of spotted muslin, warp-printed with bouquets, and trimmed with lace and threaded ribbons, has the fashionable pointed waist, pagoda sleeves and flounced skirt. The Prince wears a bow-tied cravat, and shirt with decorative studs. Patterned waistcoats were popular even, as here, with a dark, formal frock coat.

**74 The Derby Day
(detail), 1856-8
W.P. Frith**

Note (centre left) A
fashionable middle-
class young couple
dressed for a summer
day at the races.
Women's hats went
out of fashion after the
mid-1830s, but by the
late 1840s a large
round straw hat with
turned-down brim was
appearing for seaside
and country wear. By
1857 more stylish
versions, such as the
mousquetaire, were
accepted as
fashionable, but only
for the young.

Head The man wears
a top hat with the
straight sides and
almost flat brim typical
of this decade. The
young woman has a
mousquetaire hat.

Body The man's
shawl-collared
waistcoat is now cut
without the pointed
waist of the 1840s,
and with the shorter
length introduced by
1855. His dark coat is
worn with contrasting
trousers and a lighter
greatcoat. (For details
of the woman's dress,
see next illustration.)

76 The Derby Day (detail), 1856-8
W.P. Frith

Head The fashionable women wear their hair turned under at the ears, into a low-set knot. Their silk bonnets have the wider brim and sloping crown, which grew progressively smaller and slid further down the head, throughout the 1850s. The one on the right has trimmings of artificial flowers with bobbin lace on the edge and inside the brim, and round the bavolet.

Body The woman on the right has a *broderie anglaise* collar and silk day dress with pointed waist, flounced sleeves, and fringe trimming.

Accessories One woman carries a fringed parasol. Fringe trimming on dresses and accessories was popular from the mid-1840s.

75 The Derby Day (detail), 1856-8
W.P. Frith

Note As fashion demanded ever wider skirts, the usual three or four cotton petticoats were supplemented by further layers, often including one of stiff woven horsehair. Skirt flounces emphasized the horizontal line, especially when they were patterned *à disposition*.

Head The woman wears her hair in a knot and ringlets, under a striped straw hat trimmed with ruched silk ribbons and feathers and tied under the chin with wide silk ties.

Body She wears a frilled cotton collar, and a dress of cotton muslin woven with a check, the flounces printed with flowers *à disposition*. The softly pleated bodice has a pointed waist trimmed with a sash. Pagoda sleeves have separate gathered undersleeves of *broderie anglaise*. Her shawl is of lace or embroidered net.

Accessories Short gloves; heavy chain bracelet with locket; leather purse with metal frame.

open coat and waistcoat reveal a three-button shirt front, patterned cravat and braces. His fashionably checked wool trousers, with their decorative bands, have the fly fastening which had become general in the 1840s. The riding coat (left) is distinguished by its curved front edges, flapped pockets and back pleats; its wearer and the thimblerigger both wear breeches.

Accessories The riding dress is completed by the new *Napoleon* boots with their high front peak, spurs, gloves, and metal-topped cane. The youth wears boots or shoes with the wide square toes typical of this decade.

78 The Empty Purse, 1857
J. Collinson

See colour plate between pp. 96 and 97.

79 Work (detail), 1852-65
F.M. Brown

See colour plate between pp. 96 and 97.

80 Eastward Ho, 1857
After H.N. O'Neil

Note Soldiers departing for the Indian Mutiny. The dress of the officer's wife at the top of the steps is contrasted with that of the poorer working-class woman at the bottom.

Head The fashionable woman has a small bonnet set well back on the head, the poorer the wider-brimmed bonnet of the early 1850s, sparsely trimmed.

Body The fashionable woman has a mantle and flounced dress, the poorer has only the plaid wool shawl of practical working-class wear, over a dress of wool or cotton with stripes rather than flounces. The three sailors on the quay wear traditional garments, including (far left) the knitted cap (also worn by fishermen and brewers); (centre) a sou'wester hat and knitted 'jersey' or 'guernsey' jacket (worn only by seamen until the 1880s); and (right) the coarse linen shirt with braces and loose-fitting trousers or 'slops'.

Accessories The poorer woman's cloth-topped boots were common to all classes.

77 The Derby Day (detail), 1856-8
W.P. Frith

Note A group of tricksters and their victims among the crowd display the variety of contemporary styles, including (back view) fashionable riding dress; (centre – the 'thimblerigger') old-fashioned country dress; and (right – the victim of pickpockets) the dress of a fashionable youth.

Head The youth's top hat is fashionably straight-sided. Curly brims and concave sides are old-fashioned, or retained only for riding.

Body The youth wears a greatcoat with wide sleeves which echo women's pagoda sleeves. His

81 Isambard Kingdom Brunel, 1857
Photograph by Howlett

Note Although jacket and trousers are of the same tone, this is not a matching suit. The heavy wool fabrics of the mid-century sag and crease, producing a totally different look from the fashion-plate ideal.

Head His top hat is fashionably straight.

Body He wears a pointed standing collar with bow tie. His morning coat, the popular coat of the decade, is distinctive in its slightly cutaway front skirts, combined with waist seam, stitched edges, and flapped pockets. An extra buttonhole in the left lapel (for a flower) was introduced in the 1840s. He has a fashionably short waistcoat with lapels and trousers with fly front, high-set slant pockets and buttons at the outer side seams.

Accessories The wide, square-toed boots have the high toe spring typical of this decade, and stacked heels. He has a watch and chain.

82 The confidante, 1857
W. Gale

Note Jackets were fashionable informal wear in the 1850s and the style was reflected in day dresses with front-fastening jacket bodices. It was unusual to go bare-headed outdoors.

Head The confidante (left) wears her hair in ringlets beneath a fashionable feather-trimmed mousquetaire hat with a veil. Her companion has the more usual daytime hairstyle, with the hair turned under and drawn into a low chignon, with a plait across the top of the head.

Body The confidante's informal walking dress consists of a fitted jacket with pagoda sleeves, basques and decorative buttons, over a day dress open at the front, revealing a chemisette with fashionably plain, narrow collar. The undersleeves are plain and cuffed. Her companion has a simple plaid wool shawl, but her fashionably flounced skirt and lace-edged undersleeves suggest a more formal day dress.

83 Woman in day dress, 1857-60
Anon. photograph

Note In the late 1850s, the chignon was low and wide on the back of the neck, and caps, like bonnets, were worn far back on the head. Pagoda sleeves were at their widest from 1857 to 1860, necessitating fuller undersleeves, which reached to the elbow. A balloon-like form, finished with a cuff, is typical of the late 1850s and early 1860s. Front-fastening bodices usually had basques.

Head The hair is drawn back into a low flat chignon, under a cap apparently of crocheted wool or cotton.

Body She wears a *broderie anglaise* collar and a dress of lightweight silk, with front-fastening bodice and wide pagoda sleeves; the *broderie anglaise* undersleeves are separate. The dress has a pointed waist and finely pleated skirt.

Accessories Brooch, and neck chain for a watch or scent bottle.

84 Pegwell Bay (detail), 1858-9
W. Dyce

Note During the 1850s, as rail travel made visits to seaside and countryside increasingly popular, women began to adapt their dress for outdoor pursuits. These three are gathering fossils on the beach, on a chilly October day.

Head The women wear informal hats and (left) a bonnet.

Body The two on the left wear burnous mantles, the one on the right a shawl. The skirts of their day dress are tucked up into the waistband, revealing petticoats (left) probably of striped flannel, and (centre) stiff enough to suggest horsehair, or the presence of the new cage crinoline beneath. A more formal method of hitching up walking skirts was developed in the 1860s (see illustration 96.)

85 Picnic, 1859-62
Anon. engraving

Note Throughout the 1850s, fashion decreed ever wider skirts, so that increasing layers of petticoats became an intolerable burden. The solution was a hooped petticoat called a cage crinoline. Introduced from 1856, it made layers of petticoats unnecessary, although drawers were now essential. For men, full side whiskers and moustaches were popularized by the Crimean War.

Head The women wear their hair in a low chignon, braided or held in a net. They have informal hats of felt or velvet. The men wear informal hats (left) of straw, and (right) probably of felt, in the popular muffin shape.

Body The day dresses have narrow collars and tie cravats, pagoda sleeves and undersleeves, and pointed waists. Flounced skirts are worn over crinolines and drawers. The men wear informal 'lounging suits', i.e. loose jackets and matching trousers.

Accessories The women wear low-heeled ankle boots.

86 Day dress, 1862
Anon. photograph

Note Velvet was a popular trimming on plain silk, and was often echoed in hair nets of chenille. Creases betray the tight fit of the boned bodice. The pointed waist is now shorter, and was often replaced by the princess line, cut without a waist seam. High fashion preferred a plain skirt over a crinoline.

Head The woman's hair is in a low chignon, worn inside a net.

Body She wears a narrow white collar with tie and a silk day dress with velvet-trimmed bishop sleeves and cotton undersleeves. The skirt is trimmed with pinked flounces and worn over a crinoline.

Accessories These include earrings, a neck chain with attached watch or scent bottle tucked into the belt, and keys or seals hanging below.

87 Queen Victoria presenting a Bible at Windsor, 1860-2
T. Jones Barker

Note This is a ceremonial occasion on which the Queen wears court dress, here, a form of fashionable ball dress, with the addition of feather headdress and train.

Head Her hair is in a low chignon under a jewelled diadem and ostrich plumes.

Body Her silk dress has a wide décolletage edged with a lace tucker, and is trimmed with bands of silk, threaded ribbon, and lace, which merge into the short sleeves, themselves finished with a puff of lace or net. The dress has a pointed waist, and a skirt with flounces of bobbin lace (probably Honiton, since the Queen supported the dying British hand-made lace industry). The train is silk.

Accessories Across the bodice is the sash of the Order of the Garter. She wears drop earrings, pearl necklace and matching bracelets with inset cameo.

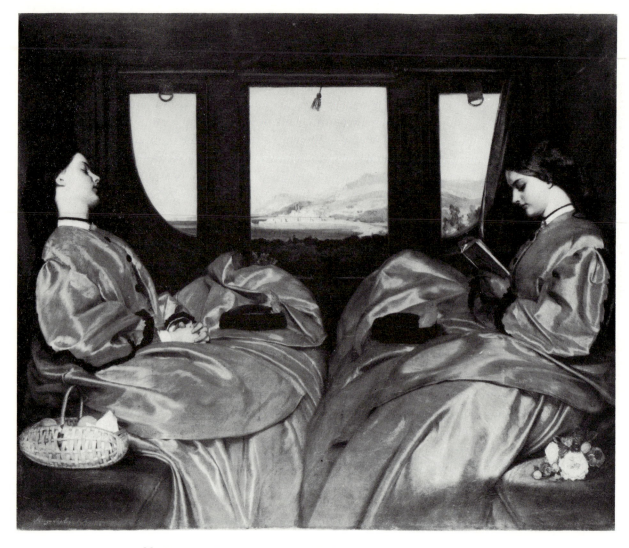

88 The Travelling Companions, 1862
A. Egg

Note Fashionable middle-class sisters, travelling through Europe, their balloon-like crinolines filling the railway carriage. When sitting, the hoops telescoped at the back, and rose slightly at the sides.

Head They wear their hair in a very large, low chignon (often supplemented by false hair).

Body They wear narrow collars. Their day dresses are worn under matching three-quarter length coats which, are loose or slightly waisted, buttoning at the front and with full, braid-trimmed sleeves (probably a paletot in contemporary terminology). They wear plain skirts over crinolines.

Accessories Ribbons with pendants are worn at the neck. On their knees are round hats of felt or velvet with turned-up brims, trimmed with a feather – a popular style for young women, often called a 'pork pie'.

89 Women in outdoor dress, 1862
H. Hilt

Note The characteristic triangular silhouette of mid-century fashion.

Head The ladies wear small sloping bonnets with high pointed brim and cut-away sides, producing the distinctive 'spoon' shape of the early 1860s (the trimmings of lace and artificial flowers inside the brim being all that is visible from the front). The flower-seller's patched suit and loose scarf proclaim his poverty. His peaked cap is of a type common to all five- to ten-year-old boys in the first half of the century.

Body The women's three-quarter length hooded cloaks of silk, fine wool or cashmere are worn over day dresses, the front one with a flounced hem. They have white undersleeves.

Accessories Short gloves and umbrellas.

90 Edward Lear, 1861-3
Photograph by McLean, Melhuish and Haes

Note Not a follower of high fashion, his clothes are still cut in the style of 1855-60. Fashion plates of the early 1860s show coats with peg-

top, rather than pagoda-shaped sleeves; peg-top trousers; and shorter waistcoats, with straight-bottomed edges, although, like his, they button high without lapels. His matching waistcoat and trousers follow the general trend towards the complete matching suit which became popular in this decade.

Head Full beard, moustache and side whiskers were increasingly common from the late 1850s.

Body He wears a bow tie, almost certainly with a standing collar; a tweed overcoat, apparently a loose paletot; and a darker cloth frock coat, distinctive by its straight front edges. The matching waistcoat and trousers are in popular fancy checked worsted.

Accessories Wide, square-toed shoes and watch chain.

92 Charles Dickens and his daughters, 1862-3
Early photograph of anon. painting

Note In the early 1860s front-fastening bodices, often with separate skirts, featured a new, higher waistline, emphasized by wide belts.

Head The girls have crimped hair in the increasingly popular high chignon, with a plait on top.

Body The day dresses have short standing collars, button fronts and bishop sleeves. The dress on the left has fashionable epaulette trimming and the wide, double-pointed Swiss belt. Both dresses have crinoline skirts. Dickens himself wears an informal turn-down shirt collar, narrow tie, and three-piece lounge suit, with inside breast pocket.

Accessories The sister on the right wears the lace-trimmed silk apron of fashionable at-home wear, and cradles a round, flower-trimmed straw hat. Both wear drop-earrings and flowers.

91 Woman's Mission: Companion of Manhood, 1863
G.E. Hicks

Note Both wear informal morning dress. Braid edgings on men's coats became a general feature from the 1850s.

Head The husband has fashionably short, side-parted hair, with long drooping 'Dundreary' side whiskers (as popularized by a character in the play *Our American Cousin* in 1861). The wife wears her hair loose at the back, although a chignon, and perhaps a morning cap, were more usual, even before breakfast.

Body The husband wears the informal three-piece lounge suit, the jacket with the narrow cuffs and high-set button typical of the 1860s. His wife's day dress is fashionably plain, with bishop sleeves (popular since 1855). She appears to wear a crinoline.

Accessories The husband's Turkish-style slippers are informal indoor wear.

**93 The Landing of H.R.H. Princess
Alexandra at Gravesend (detail), 1863**
H.N. O'Neil

Note The future Princess of Wales being
welcomed by her prospective bridegroom. Her
dress is fashionable, though simple, for the
Danish royal family had little money. The large,
dome-shaped crinoline looked best under a plain
skirt, and watered silk, or *moiré antique*, was a
popular choice.

Head and Body Her spoon-shaped bonnet has
a decorated brim, long bavolet, and wide ties.
The jacket or paletot of velvet, edged with fur, is
worn over a day dress of watered silk, with
crinoline skirt. The attendant 'maidens' wear the
loose or ringletted hair of girlhood, with
fashionable flower-trimmed straw hats, evening-
style cloaks, and crinoline dresses of white
muslin, decorated with wedding favours in the
form of ribbon rosettes.

of Chantilly, were especially prized. The crinoline of the early 1860s is flat at the front, and skirts are gored at the sides, with the back fullness extending as a short train.

Head The small, low-crowned hat of felt or straw has a ribbon rosette, an ostrich plume and a spotted net veil.

Body A black lace shawl (probably Chantilly lace) is worn over a silk day dress with fashionable epaulettes and round waist. She wears a white cotton petticoat, probably over a small crinoline.

Accessories Narrow, square-toed shoes or ankle-boots.

95 The dancing platform at Cremorn Gardens (detail)
P. Levin

See colour plate between pp. 96 and 97.

96 Queen Victoria and Princess Louise, 1865
Anon. photograph

Note Princess Louise (left) wears informal walking dress. With full crinoline skirts, jackets were either very short and bolero-shaped, in the 'Zouave' style, or hip-length, and cut very wide. Many had a ribbon trimming down the centre back. Walking skirts of the 1860s often had a series of internal cords passing from waist to hem, which, when manipulated at the waist, gathered up the skirt well clear of the mud, revealing brightly-coloured petticoats and stockings.

Head The Princess's hair is in a chignon under a round hat, probably of velvet and fur or feathers. The Queen now wears a widow's cap beneath her hooded mantle or jacket.

Body The Princess wears a jacket, probably of light wool or cashmere and a day dress, the skirt looped up to reveal a frilled petticoat over a crinoline.

94 Croquet player, 1864
G.E. Hicks

Note The contrast of black lace and white, or light-coloured, silk is characteristic of the late 1850s and early 1860s. Embroidered machine-made net was much used, but silk bobbin lace, particularly the flowing forms and clear ground

97 A widow, 1866
Anon. photograph

Note The mourning dress is fashionably cut, with its high round waist, fitted sleeves with epaulettes, and the trained skirt, which is now pleated and gored to fit the flat-fronted crinoline. A strict etiquette was followed in the choice of fabrics and colours and the duration they were worn. The white net widow's cap, with its two long streamers, and the deep crape band, were peculiar to first mourning, which lasted twelve months.

Head The hair is worn in a chignon under a widow's cap.

Body Her black silk dress is trimmed with deep bands of crape (a silk crimped to give a textured surface).

Accessories She wears black mourning jewellery, probably jet, together with commemorative lockets, and a watch and chain tucked into the belt.

98 Woman in evening dress, 1866
Photograph by Silvy

Note Pointed waists still vie with the princess line, or with a higher, rounded waist. The crinoline now has all the fullness at the back. This is emphasized by the overskirt, a form introduced in 1865, and soon to develop into a draped polonaise, worn over a bustle.

Head The hair is in a high-set chignon with ringlets.

Body The velvet dress has a slightly pointed décolletage edged with a pleated frill of net, threaded with ribbon, the bodice and puffed sleeves decorated with net, lace, and bands of velvet. She wears a lace-edged overskirt and a trained underskirt of ruched and puffed net over a crinoline.

Accessories These include drop earrings; a necklace of triple pendants in the heavy classical style, popular in this decade; a heavy chain bracelet; kid gloves; and a feather fan.

99 Interior at 'The Chestnuts', Wimbledon, 1867
J.L. Dyckmans

See colour plate between pp. 96 and 97.

100 On the Beach: a Family on Margate Sands (detail), 1867
C.W. Nichols

Note The bowler and lounge jacket, although informal, could be extremely stylish.

Head The young man has short hair, moustache and 'mutton-chop' whiskers. He wears an early form of bowler hat, a hard felt hat with distinctive bowl-shaped crown and curly brim, introduced for informal wear.

Body He has a narrow turn-down collar and neck tie. His dark cloth or velvet lounge jacket has a flower hole. He wears a fashionably short, plain, shawl-collared waistcoat and narrow trousers.

Accessories Striped stockings (also fashionable for women in this decade); short gloves; and a watch chain.

101 On the Beach (detail), 1867
C.W. Nichols

Note An innovation of this decade was the wearing of contrasting skirt and chemisette for country, 'at home' or seaside wear. The skirt often had a matching cape or jacket, forerunner of the tailor-made suit.

Head Over her high chignon, the young woman wears a straw hat with net and feather trimming and a net veil.

Body Her muslin chemisette is trimmed with lace and threaded ribbon. Beneath it are visible the low neckline and short sleeves (also ribbon-threaded) of her chemise, and across the bust, the top of her stays. She wears a Swiss belt and a silk skirt with braided hem (a protection against wear). The cotton petticoat with *broderie anglaise* hem, is probably worn over a crinoline.

Accessories These include lace-up boots; black lace shawl; short gloves with decorative points; and a silk and lace parasol.

102 An August Picnic, 1869
Anon. engraving

Head The older man wears formal day dress, including a top hat, but
more casual styles are favoured by the younger men. The one in the
foreground has a straw sailor hat, later called a boater. The man in the
centre has a protective veil, fashionable for men as well as women. The
young women wear a variety of small hats, now tilted forward to
accommodate the still rising and ever larger chignon. The girl in the right
foreground shows the fashion for loose back hair, introduced from
America in 1868.

Body and Accessories The older man's formal standing collar and frock
coat contrast with the casual lounge jackets of the younger men. The one
in the foreground may well be velvet, and is worn with fashionable braided
trousers and elastic-sided boots. The girl in the foreground has the looped
polonaise overskirt and bustle fashionable from 1868.

23 The Cloakroom,
Clifton Assembly Rooms, 1817
R. Sharples

Note Fashionable ball dress is worn here.

Head The women wear their hair in bandeaux and flowers, or under silk turbans trimmed with feathers.

Body They wear dresses of light-coloured embroidered net or lace, over brightly coloured silk or satin underdresses, featuring the puffed sleeves and very high waists of 1815-20. The flared skirts have deep flounced or vandyked hems, often trimmed with artificial flowers. The men wear white cravats and waistcoats, dark dress coats and breeches or pantaloons.

Accessories The women's accessories include low-heeled satin shoes, long kid gloves, shawls and fans. The new arrival (seated right), is still removing her fur-edged overshoes. The men wear lace-up pumps, except for the two on the left, whose military uniforms demand hessian boots.

78 The Empty Purse
1857
J. Collinson

Note This is a fashionable middle-class woman at a bazaar.

Head Her bonnet is fashionably sloped and foreshortened to frame the head and reveal the trimmings of ruched net and flowers inside the brim. It has wide ribbon ties and a spotted silk bonnet veil.

Body She wears a silk dress with an unusual V-front, over a chemisette. The dress has a pointed waist; flounced pagoda-shaped undersleeves of muslin, threaded with ribbon; and a skirt with fashionable pinked flounces, striped *a disposition*.

Accessories She wears short kid gloves and holds a beaded stocking purse and one of its rings. On the stand is a woman's hat, trimmed with ribbons and feathers. Also visible are a pair of men's braces (above), and (left) a worked pattern for men's slippers, both hand-embroidered in wool.

79 Work (detail), 1852-65
F.M. Brown

Note This painting shows the range of London society, including a rare depiction of navvies.

Head The foreman (right) has a tasselled cap of a type commonly worn by small boys. The man on the left has a simple stocking cap, traditional headwear for working men, particularly sailors and brewers.

Body and Accessories The foreman's coarse linen shirt is cut like its fashionable counterparts, with low-set, full gathered sleeves. He follows fashion with a bow tie, fancy waistcoat and watch and chain under his linen apron. His men wear typical working clothes, including loose shirts or a plain smock (centre); old-fashioned breeches or cord trousers (left), hitched up at the knee with 'yarks'; thick woollen stockings; and lace-up 'blucher' boots. The two middle-class women (left) are dressed in the fashions of the late 1850s.

**95 The Dancing Platform at Cremorne
Gardens (detail) 1864**
P. Levin

Note Expensively dressed ladies of the town in
the popular pleasure gardens. Crinolines are still
very large, but with more fullness at the back.
This is emphasized by the use of basques and
shaped overskirts, which by 1868 will have
developed into bustles and pannier skirts.

Head To offset wide crinoline skirts, headwear
is small and neat, whether it be a narrow-brimmed
hat (left), the popular 'spoon' bonnet (centre), or
an unusual toque (right).

Body The woman in the centre wears a lace
mantle with an attached cape over her silk day
dress, the contrasts of dark plain silk and pale
lace being particularly fashionable in this
decade. The woman on the left has a silk dress
overlaid with multi-puffed sleeves and a draped
overskirt of paler tulle or net. The third dress
features a bodice with sash-like basques at the
back, and a separate overskirt with cutaway
sides.

99 Interior at 'The Chestnuts', Wimbledon, 1867
J.L. Dyckmans

Note Middle-class women in formal day dress.

Head The younger woman has fashionably crimped hair in a high chignon, tied with ribbon. The older married woman, as befits her age and status, wears a dress cap (although these confections of lace, net and ribbons were usually smaller and less enveloping by this decade).

Body The younger woman wears a dress of watered silk, with front-buttoning bodice, belted waist, shoulder trimming and the shaped sleeves which finally replaced bishop sleeves. Her skirt is gored and pleated to give a flat front and a train, now supported by a half-crinoline or by petticoats only. The child wears a dress of stiffened muslin over a miniature round crinoline, and the front-lacing boots with small heels which were also being introduced for adult wear.

Accessories A fashionably heavy brooch and fringed drop earrings are worn by the younger woman.

106 **The Fair Toxophilites 1872**
W.P. Frith

Note The artist's daughters in fashionable day dress. Mauve was one of the aniline dyes first developed in 1856. It remained fashionable until the mid-1870s.

Head Their hair is in heavy plaited chignons. Hats of felt and/or velvet are trimmed with ribbons and lace veiling (left) or feathers.

Body They wear lace-edged collars and jabots. The dress on the left has pagoda sleeves and basques at the back. The bustle is emphasized by the layered sash, basques and the overskirt, which is draped to give an apron front and a pannier at the back. The dress on the right has a bodice with attached overskirt and contrasting flounced skirt.

107 Too Early (detail), 1873
J. Tissot

Note London society girls in full ball dress.
Evening dresses of the early 1870s were frothy
confections. Pastel silks became misty seen
through overskirts and frills of white muslin, net
or gauze. Bustles, panniers and trains gave an
undulating line, softened by pleated frills, lace
flounces, ruched ribbons, and flower sprays.

Head They have fringed or centrally-parted
hair in high plaited chignons, decorated with
flowers, ribbons or feathers.

Body Their low-necked, short-sleeved dresses
have high, round waists, draped overskirts and
trained skirts, the fullness set in pleats at the
back and supported by a bustle.

Accessories Velvet ribbons decorate necks and
wrists. Kid evening gloves are still short, and
fans large.

136 St Martin-in-the-Fields (detail) 1888
W. Logsdail

Note Middle-class woman and child in
fashionable winter outdoor dress. The tall-
crowned, flower-pot shaped 'post-boy' hat was
one of the most popular of the decade, matching
the overall silhouette with its narrow angular
forms. The 1880s and 1890s saw the importation
of thousands of exotic birds which appeared on
fashionable fans and headwear as plumes, wings,
or even whole birds. Dark reds were typical of
the late 1870s and 1880s.

Head The woman wears her hair in a knot
under a tall 'post-boy' hat, probably of felt or
beaver, trimmed with silk ribbon and feathers.

Body She wears a sheath-like cloth coat edged
with fur over a dress with a bustle.

Accessories She has high-heeled shoes or
boots with pointed toes, gloves and an umbrella.

103 Day dress, 1870
Anon. photograph

Note Light colours trimmed with dark braid or piping, together with fringes and narrow pleated flounces, are characteristic of 1868-75. Square necklines and yokes were fashionable from 1868. The waistband and overskirt may be attached to the bodice (i.e. a polonaise) or may be worn as a separate garment. It was usual to match the bow at the front with a larger version at the back, to emphasize the bustle.

Head The hair is worn in a high chignon with loose ringlets at the back.

Body The jacket bodice has pagoda sleeves and undersleeves. The overskirt is cut in handkerchief points. The short, walking-length skirt is apparently worn over a narrow crinoline or half-crinoline, and a bustle.

Accessories She wears a brooch and a heavy necklace.

104 The Marchioness of Huntley, 1870
Sir John Everett Millais

Note The Marchioness avoids fashion extremes to achieve romantic simplicity. Her square neckline and high round waistline are typical of 1868-74, although her epaulettes are no longer high fashion by 1870. The skirt, with its flat front, gored sides and long train, shows the transitional stage between crinoline and bustle. Here it is worn without either, but the trimmings suggest the more fashionable alternative of an apron-fronted overskirt, which high fashion would have worn draped and puffed over a bustle and half crinoline.

Head Her hair is in a high but plain chignon trimmed with ribbons.

Body Her summer day dress of muslin is trimmed with threaded silk ribbons and lace.

Accessories She wears drop earrings, a neck ribbon with a pearl drop pendant, and a bracelet. Her gloves are probably of very soft leather.

107 Too Early (detail), 1873
J. Tissot

See colour plate between pp. 96 and 97.

105 The Marquess of Townshend, 1870
Anon. caricature

Note The straight 'chimney pot' top hat of the mid century was reduced in height after 1865, while the years 1869-76 saw a fashion for very short coats, their hems, like this one, well above the knee. The artist exaggerates the waisted effects, however, and has missed out the waist seam.

Head Moustache and side whiskers were both fashionable in this decade. Beards were general for older men. He wears a top hat.

Body He has a turn-down collar with narrow tie; a pale waistcoat; a double-breasted 'top frock' overcoat with silk-faced lapels and breast pocket. His trousers have gaiter bottoms, a popular alternative to the narrow cut.

Accessories Fashionable square-toed shoes and tasselled cane.

106 The Fair Toxophilites, 1872
W.P. Frith

See colour plate between pp. 96 and 97.

108 Mrs Bischoffsheim, 1873
Sir John Everett Millais

Note She wears formal afternoon or dinner dress. A flowered bodice with sleeve ruffles and panniers, worn with a flounced underskirt, was a fashionable revival of the polonaise robe and petticoat of the 1770s. The bow-trimmed front panel recalls the stomacher. This is a dressier version of the chintz 'Dolly Varden' bodices of 1871-2.

Head The hair is in a full chignon, trimmed with ribbons or lace.

Body The square-necked jacket bodice of brocaded silk is trimmed with lace, the front cuffs and turn-back panels in plain silk, matching the flounced skirt. The overskirt is draped in panniers, the whole dress worn over a bustle.

Accessories She has pearl earrings and pendant on a velvet ribbon, long kid gloves and a fan.

109 **The Ball on Shipboard (detail), 1874**
J. Tissot

Note For this daytime event at Henley Regatta both formal and informal
day dress are acceptable.

Head The men wear informal straw sailor hats, or curly-brimmed
bowlers. The women have full braided chignons with forward-tilted straw
sailor hats, or more formal bonnets at the new backward-tilted angle.

Body The tight jacket bodices with basques are worn with draped, apron-
fronted overskirts, puffed at the back over a bustle. The figure coming up
the stairs wears the newly introduced cuirass bodice, which fits tightly over
the hips, and the ruffled, elbow-length sleeves of formal dress.

Accessories Some of the men have two-tone brogue shoes, popular for
informal wear.

100

110 Travelling scene, 1874
Anon. engraving

Note A middle-class couple dressed for travelling.

Head The fashionable wife wears her hair in a full chignon, with an exaggeratedly small, forward-tilted hat. Her husband has full side whiskers and the curved and curly-brimmed top hat of the first half of the 1870s.

Body He wears a greatcoat or paletot over his cut-away morning coat and waistcoat. She wears fashionable day dress, the square-necked jacket bodice with slightly pagoda-shaped sleeves and ruffles, the skirts draped to give an apron front and puffed back. Her matching underskirt has a flounced hem and train, supported by a bustle.

111 The Ulster, 1874
G.F. Watts

Head Hair drawn back into a high chignon.
Forward-tilted hat, probably of hard felt,
trimmed with feathers. The hat is very plain and
masculine in style, suitable for informal walking
or travelling.

Body She wears an Ulster coat, an overcoat
worn by both sexes and also called a 'waterproof',
'dust-cloak', or 'travelling wrap'. The female
version was distinctive for its fitted waist, shaped
by darts, or pulled in by a half belt, and for its
length (some were cut with a train). Many, like
this one, had a detachable hood. The male
version usually featured a hood and a belt.

112 The Dinner Hour, Wigan, 1874
E. Crowe

Note The dress of women working in the textile mills of the industrial North makes few concessions to the fashionable ideal.

Head Long hair is secured in a net for practicality and safety.

Body The basic dress consists of a short-sleeved linen overall with draw-string neck and open back, worn over chemise, stays and coarse linen or woollen petticoats. No bustles are worn (although in the 1860s many factory girls had worn crinolines).

Accessories Most wear wooden-soled leather clogs with metal clasps. Some have stockings of coarse wool or cotton. Others go without – 'slip-shod'. Simple plaid wool shawls are cheap and practical, and can be drawn over the head to form a hood. A few wear drop-earrings and necklaces, perhaps of glass or wood.

113 Poor Relations (detail), 1875
G.G. Kilburne

Note The years 1874-5 saw the introduction of
the cuirass bodice, which extended in sheath-like
form over the hips, making the bustle impossible.
The fullness in the back of the skirt slipped
downwards, in waterfall draperies, producing, in
a few years, a narrow, tie-back skirt with a train.
Here, the middle-class daughter of the house
demonstrates the transitional stage.

Head The hair is worn in a simple plaited
chignon.

Body The day dress consists of a bodice with
cuirass front but a high-waisted polonaise form
at the sides, which appears to be looped up
towards the back, still giving the effect of a
bustle. She has a lace or muslin neck frill and
long sleeves with frilled mousquetaire cuffs. The
flounced skirt may be tied back, but is still fairly
full.

Accessories She wears low-heeled shoes with
pointed toes.

114 Poor Relations (detail), 1875
G.G. Kilburne

Note The impoverished middle-class girl is
dressed neatly, with all the essential accessories,
but is too poor to follow fashion, except in the
style and angle of her hat.

Head Her hair is in a chignon, under a round
hat set on the back of the head.

Body Her day dress is of silk or wool (its
plainness suggests that it is home-made, or a
hand-me-down, perhaps worn by her mother in
the 1860s). The well-to-do child wears a silk
dress with basque bodice and sash, simulating a
bustle; a linen overall and stockings with fancy
clocks.

Accessories The young woman has an
inexpensive checked wool shawl, short gloves of
unfashionably thick leather, and a plain umbrella.
The child wears low-heeled shoes with the
pointed toes and decorative rosettes that are also
fashionable adult wear.

115 Day dress, 1875-7

Anon. photograph

Note This mixing of cuirass, princess and polonaise forms is typical of 1875-85, when dress construction was highly complex. The chief aim was to offset the narrow vertical line with graceful draperies.

Head The hair is worn in a neat braided chignon.

Body She wears a dress of contrasting materials, probably silk and velvet. The bodice front appears to be continuous with the skirt in the princess style, with the velvet side pieces extending as a long polonaise overskirt. The panel on the skirt front is draped in the fashionable apron shape, emphasizing the cuirass effect of the bodice. The back of the skirt is slightly puffed and gathered, the remnant of the bustle, but with the fullness extending as a train.

116 Woman in day dress, 1876
J. Tissot

Note By 1876 the overall silhouette was sheath-like, the bustle giving way to a waterfall of drapery extending as a train. Trimmings of flounces, pleats and ruching became more elaborate as the decade progressed.

Head The curly-brimmed hat is decorated with feathers (probably ostrich).

Body The dress of striped muslin, trimmed with silk bows, has a short polonaise bodice, the frilled edge forming the fashionable high standing collar and frilled cuffs. There is a separate overskirt with frilled edge dipping down at the back and a flounced underskirt.

Accessories A large, plain parasol was a fashionable alternative to those with lace edgings or trimmings of ribbon bows or ruchings.

117 The Gallery of HMS *Calcutta* (detail), 1876
J. Tissot

Note In the most fashionable dresses, bodices are carefully seamed to fit like sheaths, while draping and elaborate frills produce a waterfall effect in the skirt.

Head Hair is worn in long braided chignons under a curly-brimmed silk bonnet (left) and a hat (right), decorated with ribbons on the outside and flowers or pleated net under the brim.

Body The day dresses of silk (left) and striped muslin (right), have high frilled collars of lace or net. The long polonaise bodices are in princess style, tied and draped at the back under ribbon bows and frills. The matching tie-back skirts are decorated with rows of frills (those on the left are pinked), the fullness gathered at the back in a short train.

Accessories Fans are becoming larger, reaching up to sixteen inches in length in the 1880s.

118 Day dress, 1876-8
Anon. photograph

Note Contrasting materials were frequently used to emphasize the narrow, vertical line of the body and to give a cuirass effect, even in jacket bodices. Similarly, the fashion for asymmetrical skirt draperies is imitated in bands of trimming. Concealed pockets were no longer feasible in such narrow skirts, and the years 1876-8 saw a brief fashion for large, decorative pockets, set low on the skirt.

Head The parted hair is drawn into a neat, low chignon.

Body Her dress is of contrasting materials, probably silk and velvet. She wears a simple jacket bodice, narrow white collar and cuffs, a tie-back skirt with flapped pocket, and a train decorated with bows.

Accessories She has a heavy brooch and pendant. Her watch chain is tucked into the bodice front.

119 The Arrest, 1877
After W.P. Frith

Note The bailiffs serve a writ on the upper-class gambler. He and his family wear informal morning dress.

Head The husband has fashionably parted hair and moustache. His wife wears an oval-shaped 'Charlotte Corday' morning cap of muslin, lace and ribbon.

Body The husband's standing collar and necktie are those of formal day dress, but at present worn beneath a patterned dressing-gown, probably of thick wool, with contrasting shawl collar and cuffs, cord tie and edgings. His wife has a princess-style dressing gown or informal morning robe, with high collar and lace-edged front opening. The girl wears her silk day dress under a linen or cotton overall. The boy has a velvet knickbocker suit.

120 Evening dress, 1877-80
Anon. photograph

Note Although a simple chignon was now usual for daytime, full ringlets were often retained for evening. The squarish neckline, stomacher-like front, sleeve ruffles and delicate jewellery, particularly the pendant brooch, are all features consciously revived from the eighteenth century, a period much copied throughout the 1870s and early 1880s.

Head The hair is in a chignon with long back ringlets, decorated probably with lace or feathers.

Body Her dress is of contrasting materials, probably silk and velvet, edged with lace. The cuirass bodice has contrasting panels forming a stomacher front, and lacing together down the centre. The heart-shaped neckline is edged with a frill of lace or pleated net. There is a seperate, tie-back skirt with vandyked hem, and a separate or attached overskirt, extending as a train.

121 Two women in day dress, 1878
Photograph by Elliot and Fry

Note Skirts were now so sheath-like that long stays were essential, and combinations were introduced to dispense with the bulk of separate chemise and drawers. Petticoats were few and narrow, with extra flounces at the back to support the fall of drapery which replaced the bustle from 1876-80.

Head They wear their hair in chignons under (left) a hard felt Tyrolean hat, trimmed with ribbons and a bird's wing, and (right) a soft-crowned toque, trimmed with feathers.

Body Both wear a narrow white collar and a dress in the form of a princess-style polonaise, with narrow cuffed sleeves, a centre-front opening decorated with bows, and a tie-back skirt with back draperies and train. The pleated flounces at the hem may belong to a separate underskirt, but more probably are attached directly to the lining of the main skirt.

110

122 Couple in formal day dress, 1878
Photograph by Elliot and Fry

Note For both sexes the fashionable head is small and neat, the body tall and slender.

Head The woman wears her hair in the increasingly popular frizzed fringe and a plaited chignon.

Body Her polonaise dress, in the princess style, with a tie-back skirt, gives a narrow line, emphasized by narrow sleeves and the ruched panel in contrasting material down the centre front. Both the dress and the plain silk underskirt are draped at the back to give a train. His narrow winged collar and bow tie are almost hidden by his high buttoning frock coat, its straight cut echoed by narrow sleeves and trousers. (The outside breast pocket went out of fashion in 1877.)

Accessories Her high frilled collar is finished with a black lace jabot. She carries a fashionably large feather-trimmed fan with a tasselled cord. She may have a chatelaine bag on the cord around her waist.

123 A railway smoking saloon, 1879
Anon. engraving

Note Cigarette smoking became popular for men during the Crimean War. 'Fast' young ladies also indulged, but respectable women generally objected to the smell of smoke on clothing, encouraging their menfolk to adopt special caps and jackets for the purpose. The caps were always pill-box shaped, made of silk, wool or velvet, and often embroidered by their loved ones in vaguely Turkish patterns. The typical jacket was easy-fitting, with a quilted silk collar, and decorated with braid or frogging. Both were popular till the end of the century.

Head and Body The men wear informal day dress consisting of narrow standing or (right) turn-down collar, and lounge suits with very high buttoning jackets and waistcoats. The man on the right wears a smoking cap with button and hanging tassel.

124 **Scarborough Spa at Night, 1879**
F.S. Muschamp

Head The women wear small hats or toques, trimmed with flowers and feathers, or high-crowned hat with birds' wings. The men favour the tall, straight-sided, small-brimmed top hats of the late 1870s, or bowler hats, both high- and low-crowned.

Body The princess polonaise is the most popular dress, decorated with bows and pleated frills. The woman on the right loops up her train for walking. On a warm summer night, lace shawls are the most popular outerwear, tied fichu-style (right). The men wear high-buttoning frock coats or overcoats. The little boy has the long hair more usually associated with aesthetic dress, and a sailor hat and suit with knickerbockers.

125 Aesthetic dress, 1879
G. du Maurier

Note In artistic circles in the late 1870s the extremes of high fashion were rejected in favour of 'aesthetic dress'. For women this meant romantically loose hair, loose dresses worn without stays or stiffened petticoats, and large puffed sleeves in the Renaissance style. For children, it was mixed with a revival of early nineteenth-century fashions, as depicted in the drawings of Kate Greenaway.

Head The fashionable girls on the right wear adult-style hats but the aesthetic children favour old-fashioned, wide-brimmed bonnets.

Body The fashionable mother wears a polonaise dress, and her daughters' princess-style coats follow the same line. The aesthetic girls have shoulder capes and high-waisted printed cotton dresses as popular between 1810 and 1830. The older girl's puffed sleeves are typical of aesthetic dress.

Accessories Peacock feathers and sunflowers were favourite aesthetic motifs.

127 Couple in aesthetic dress, 1880
G. du Maurier

Note Among aesthetes, exotically embroidered or brocaded silks in the 'Renaissance' style were an alternative to the soft oriental silks in the muted 'greenery-yallery' colours, which they obtained at Liberty's.

Head The man's long hair and clean-shaven face brand him as an aesthete, as does the woman's loose, frizzed hair, in the style popularized by the Pre-Raphaelite painters.

Body The man's turn-down collar, soft tie, and lounge jacket (probably of velvet with a quilted silk collar), are fashionable informal dress, although velvet jackets were particularly associated with aestheticism. The woman's dress, probably of brocaded silk, has the low neck, puffed 'Renaissance' sleeves, lack of waist seam and loose, flowing skirt typical of aesthetic gowns.

126 Day dress, 1879-81
Anon. photograph

Note After 1878 hems rose and trains became less fashionable, leaving skirts as straight tubes, smothered with horizontal bands of ruches, puffs and narrow-pleated frills. In the early 1880s, the upper skirt was often curved to form panniers over the hips.

Head Her toque is swathed in ostrich feathers.

Body The cuirass bodice is probably of the popular Genoa velvet (a satin ground, patterned with a velvet pile). She wears a narrow, standing collar, and fancy buttons; jabot and frilled cuffs, probably of lace or muslin; and a contrasting skirt, the upper front arranged in horizontal pleats and a pleated frill, the back arranged in vertical pleats and slightly puffed.

Accessories She carries a Japanese paper parasol. The flow of Japanese imports produced by the 1868 revolution reached new levels in the 1880s.

OSCAR WILDE.
Copyright 1882, by N. Sarony.
NEW YORK.

128 Oscar Wilde, 1882
Photograph by Sarony

Note Photographed in New York, when Wilde was on his famous lecture tour of the United States. Aesthetes and dress reformers favoured the mediaeval forms of men's dress, consisting of a loose tunic and knee-breeches. Wilde himself admired cavalier dress, and from 1880 wore his version (velvet jackets and breeches) to evening parties. The breeches and stockings shown here were bought from a theatrical costumier especially for the tour.

Head Wilde has aesthetic-style long hair and a clean-shaven face.

Body and Accessories He wears an informal turn-down collar and unfashionably large silk tie; a double-breasted cloth lounge or smoking jacket with quilted silk collar and cuffs, and decorative frogging; knee-breeches with silk stockings; and flat or low-heeled shoes with wide ribbon ties.

129 Outdoor dress, 1883-6
Anon. photograph

Note The soft leather of the gloves outlines the cuffs of the shorter sleeve introduced in 1883. The panniers of the early 1880s have now filled out and softened as the skirt widens to incorporate the new bustle. Woollen walking outfits like this one are plainer in style than more formal day dresses, and set the trend for the more tailored lines of the second half of the decade.

Head The hat of fur or beaver is trimmed with ostrich feathers.

Body The cravat of figured net is tucked into the bodice front to give a plastron effect. She wears a day dress, probably of wool, with a cuirass bodice; a separate overskirt, draped in panniers over the hips and back; and a straight skirt with the back arranged in vertical pleats over a bustle.

Accessories She carries a fur muff and wears gloves, probably kid.

130 Marion Hood, 1884
Photograph by Elliot and Fry

Note This is fashionable formal day dress, the draperies of which were at their most exuberant in the mid-1880s, just before they disappeared almost entirely.

Head She wears her hair with a fringe (fashionable sine 1882), and a loose version of the low-set chignon.

Body The velvet bodice has a standing collar, fashionably short sleeves and a pointed front waist, with a lace neck frill, sleeve ruffles and plastron. The silk skirt, with train, is made up from panels of draped and ruched silk, intermingled with swags and frills of lace, attached to a plain lining, which is tied with tapes inside the back, and worn over a bustle.

Accessories She wears a necklace, possibly of amber, and kid or suede gloves. Her fancy-mesh, machine-knit stockings probably match the dress. Her shoes are of fancy leather, with pointed toes, decorative rosettes, and probably one-and-a-half to two-inch heels.

117

132 Lady Dilke, 1887
H. von Herkomer

Note An artist's version of fashionable ball dress. (Compare this with the contemporary photograph in the previous plate.) The second half of the decade saw a slow return to a narrow vertical line, and the gradual decrease of the bustle. From 1887 straight pleats replaced apron draperies in skirts. Here, the gathered shoulder 'kick-up' of 1889 is already predicted in the ribbon bows on the sleeves.

Head The hair is swept up to a knot on the crown.

Body She wears a dress of silk figured with flowers in eighteenth-century style, with asymmetrical draperies of silk and heavy lace. The heavily-boned bodice has a low V-neck front and back. The skirt hangs straight at the front, the sides tied back over a bustle and extending as a train.

Accessories She is holding long evening gloves.

131 Ball dress, 1886
Anon. photograph

Note A V-shaped or heart-shaped décolletage was the most fashionable for ball dresses by the mid-1880s, and coupled with the sheath-like bodice and vestigial sleeves, gave a vertical emphasis and a starkness echoed in the cap-like hairstyle. Gloves reaching to, or even above, the elbow fastened with up to twenty buttons.

Head The hair is dressed in a tightly curled fringe, and a small knot on the crown, a style often decorated with flowers or feathers.

Body The heavily-boned bodice has a low V-neck front and back, emphasized with pleated net. Her skirt has a draped apron front and puffed and gathered back, worn over a bustle, and probably extending as a train.

Accessories The gloves would be of silk, kid or suede. She has cameo brooches and fashionably heavy bangles (now worn over the gloves).

133 The First Cloud, 1887
Sir William Quiller Orchardson

Note This upper-class couple are in full evening dress. The bustle of the 1880s was much narrower and more angular than that of the 1870s, and when worn with a train, gave a greater sense of movement.

Head The woman wears her hair swept into a knot, with flower or feather trimming.

Body Her silk gown has the extreme décolletage and vestigial sleeves typical of the late 1880s. Her draped tie-back skirt is worn over a bustle. The man has the fashionable standing collar, white bow tie, starched shirt front and cutaway dress coat (although by the mid-1880s lapels were generally superseded by the roll collar for evening).

134 Will it Rain? 1887
J. Charles

Note An old country woman in unfashionable outdoor dress. Without the appropriate substructure of crinoline or bustle, there is little to date a simple, working-class dress. Shawls went out of fashion with the demise of the crinoline, but remained popular among the poorer classes. This one probably dates from before 1840, when they became larger and more densely patterned.

Head The parted hair is drawn into a knot. The black bonnet has the slightly raised brim, trimmings on top of the crown, and wide ribbon ties most fashionable in the early 1880s.

Body She wears a shawl with fringed and patterned border, pinned at the front. Her dress, probably of inexpensive printed cotton, has an unfashionably simple gathered skirt, worn without a bustle.

Accessories Large, practical apron, umbrella and shopping basket.

135 Sir Arthur Sullivan, 1888
Sir John Everett Millais

Note Sir Arthur wears fashionable formal day dress. Coats were buttoned very high in this decade. Collars, shirt fronts, and cuffs were heavily starched in the latter half of the century.

Head He has short hair, probably sleeked with macassar oil (a side-parting was equally fashionable). Moustaches were usual, with or without short side whiskers.

Body He wears a winged collar and unusually wide tie; a double-breasted frock coat with cuffs; stiffened shirt cuffs; and contrasting trousers.

Accessories A monocle hangs from a cord round his neck, a popular accessory since the 1850s, and particularly associated with fops and 'swells'.

136 St Martin-in-the-Fields (detail), 1888
W. Logsdail

See colour plate between pp. 96 and 97.

137 Frances Hodgson Burnett, 1888
Anon. photograph

Note The Anglo-American authoress of *Little Lord Fauntleroy*, wears an evening dress in Grecian style. Classical robes were admired by the aesthetes for their artistic flowing lines, and by dress reformers for their healthy lack of constriction. In her imitation of classical draperies she rejects the separate bodice and skirt, although the draperies follow fashionable lines in the cross-over bodice, and skirt with apron front, bustle and train. She appears to be wearing stays and fashionable lace-trimmed petticoats.

Head Her frizzled hair, has a low 'aesthetic' fringe.

Body The dress of light silk is applied to a firm lining. The short sleeves have lacings, which are a classical motif. The hem is trimmed with applied braid in a pattern reminiscent of the Grecian key design.

Accessories She wears a simple pearl necklace and carries a fashionably large feather fan, decorated with a whole bird or bird wing.

138 A Royal Academy Private View (detail), 1888-9
H.J. Brooks

Head The standing women wear their hair swept back into a high-set knot, beneath (left) a tall pointed hat, and (right) a bonnet trimmed with feathers and ribbons. The seated woman (left), shows the fashionable tilt of the bonnet, with its cut-out back revealing the hair.

Body and Accessories Over their day dresses, with fitted bodices and bustle skirts, the women wear (left) a fur boa, and (right) a fur mantle, cut in the style of the late 1880s, with its wide sleeves and long pointed fronts, descending from a short flared back, which rests on the bustle. This woman also carries a be-ribboned fur muff, a popular winter accessory for most of the century. The men wear the ubiquitous silk top hats and frock coats.

139 Dulcie Delight and the Curate, 1889
Anon. engraving

Note A middle-class country girl in a tailor-made costume (originally informal outdoor dress and now fashionable morning wear). In very fashionable dresses, this year saw the bustle reduced to a mere pad.

Head She wears her hair in a knot under a be-ribboned straw hat, in shape half way between a 'post-boy' and a wide-brimmed 'Gainsborough'. The curate's flat hat is typical clerical wear.

Body Her dress is probably of light wool or flannel, trimmed with plain cloth or velvet (stripes were very popular in the late 1880s). The high standing collar is typical of 1880-1900. The dress has a mock waistcoat front with lapels, a variant of the plastron. Three-quarter-length sleeves were fashionable from 1883, and here they have the slightly gathered shoulders of 1889, the beginnings of a new gigot sleeve. Her simple draped skirt, a feature of the tailor-made is worn over a bustle.

140 City day dress, 1890
Anon. engraving

Note A middle-class couple in simple, conservative, outdoor dress.

Head The woman has a fashionable frizzed fringe and high-set knot of hair, under a toque trimmed with ribbons and a bird's wing. The man wears a semi-formal felt hat.

Body The woman's fitted jacket is a less dressy alternative to the popular mantle, and is probably made of cloth trimmed with darker fabric or fur. Her day dress has a simple draped skirt worn over a bustle. The man wears a Chesterfield overcoat (distinctive by its straight lines and outside pockets).

Accessories Her reticule or dress bag is probably home-made, for during the 1880s soft drawstring bags were being superseded by commercially-made leather handbags with metal frames and fastenings, more stylish versions of the man's travelling bag.

141 The Countess of Aberdeen, 1891
Anon. photograph

Note The Countess wears formal day dress. The bustle has now disappeared, leaving a flared skirt with back pleats. Jackets were popular with skirts and dresses, in either matching or contrasting fabrics.

Head Her hair is swept high into a knot, under a velvet bonnet trimmed with flowers, tying with a velvet bow.

Body The high-collared bodice is of dark fabric, probably silk, with an unusual inset pleated panel in a lighter colour, and a high waist sash. The fitted jacket of silk or cloth has the gathered shoulders typical of the early 1890s. The skirt is shaped and gored to hang straight at the front, with pleats at the back. Trimming of applied braid in scrolling patterns was popular from the 1880s.

Accessories She wears short day gloves and a chatelaine hangs from her waist.

142 The Royal Academy Conversazione (detail), 1891
G. Manton

Note The guests wear fashionable evening dress. From 1889-92, the main emphasis in female dress was vertical, particularly at the shoulder.

Head The women's hair is arranged with a fringe or centre parting and a high knot, to create a small neat head, undecorated except perhaps for an ornamental comb.

Body Sleeves are cut with a kick-up at the shoulder (fashionable from 1889). Even the shoulder straps of the full evening dress (left) have vertically arranged frills. Waists may be round or pointed. Bustles are no longer worn, although trains are still retained for evening. The shadow on the bodice of the woman on the right reveals the line of her stays.

Accessories Fashionable accessories are elbow-length gloves of kid or suede, and very large fans.

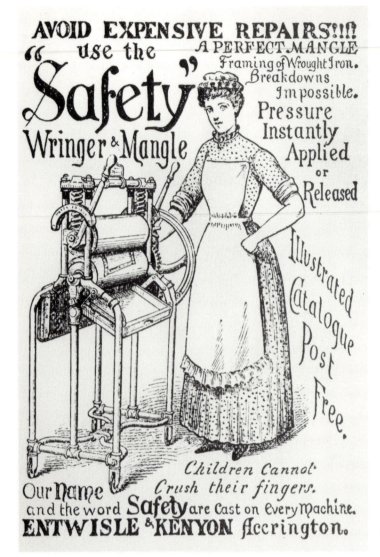

144 Woman in walking dress, 1893
Anon. photograph

Note The blouse became increasingly fashionable in the 1890s, but, whether frilly or plain, its apparent informality was belied by its heavily boned lining. It was worn with a simple skirt or, outdoors, a tailor-made costume. For walking, cycling and sports, masculine styles were adopted.

Head Her frizzed hair is in a knot. The coarse straw sailor hat, trimmed with silk ribbon, is worn fashionably flat on the head.

Body The blouse has a high standing collar and masculine tie. Her tailor-made costume is of checked wool. The jacket has the wide gigot sleeves of 1893-7, emphasized by wide lapels. She wears a waistcoat with the still fashionable pointed waist and a plain gored skirt with waist darts.

Accessories Short day gloves and fashionably heavy charm bracelets.

143 Magazine advertisement, 1892
Anon. engraving

Note The kitchen maid wears the basic uniform of female domestic servants – frilled cap, cheap printed cotton dress and apron. Although her outfit is plain and simple in construction, it reflects high fashion in the following features.

Head Her hair is worn in a knot on the crown. Her small cap is worn, like fashionable hats, flat on top of the head.

Body Her dress has a high collar, front-fastening bodice, narrow sleeves (although without the fashionable gathered shoulder), round waist at natural level and a skirt supported only by petticoats, with the fullness at the back. A more expensive skirt would be gored and pleated rather than gathered.

Accessories Her shoes have slight heels and pointed toes.

145 Middle-class couple, holidaying in the country, 1894
Anon. engraving

Note Their dress is smart but informal.

Head The woman wears her hair frizzed and probably padded, in a heavy knot or coil. Her wide-brimmed hat is trimmed with either ribbon bows or bird's wings. Her husband wears the soft, peaked cap which was originally sportswear, but popular in the 1890s for general leisure activities.

Body The woman wears a contrasting jacket and skirt, probably with a blouse. Fashionable features are the high standing collar, gigot sleeves and applied trimmings of braid or ribbon. The cut of the skirt is typical of 1890-7, when gores and darts gave a snug fit on the hips, while deep pleats, cut on the cross, gave a flowing line at the back. The man's lounge suit displays the large checks often used for informal suits in this decade.

146 Mother and daughter, 1895
Anon. engraving

Note The women wear fashionable outdoor dress. Sleeves were at their widest in this year, making capes, cloaks and mantles the most popular outer garments.

Head The daughter wears her waved or frizzed hair in a low knot under a boat-shaped hat, trimmed with birds' wings, or a whole bird in flight, and a spotted veil. Her mother wears a bonnet (now favoured only by older women) decorated with large upstanding bows and a spotted veil.

Body Both wear high-collared day dresses, the daughter's demonstrating the fashionable gigot sleeves and a flared skirt. Her mother's cape is made of silk or cloth decorated with braid and ribbon, and edged with fur or beaded braid.

Accessories Both have fashionably long parasols, and the daughter's shoes or boots show the current style of pointed toes and high heels.

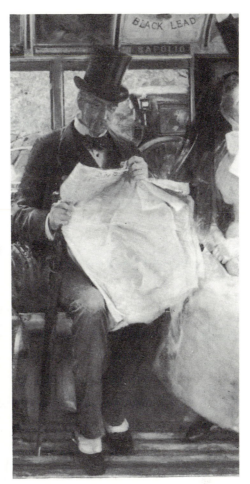

147 The Bayswater Omnibus (detail), 1895
T.M. Joy

Note The large gigot sleeves of the middle of
the decade were matched by broad-collared
capes or cloaks, and wide-brimmed 'picture'
hats. Clear stones were popular for tiny brooches
and pins, in the form of crescents, stars, hearts,
birds and animals. Some fastened pendant
watches.

Head and Body The fashionable woman,
dressed for city travelling, wears a wide-brimmed
hat, a high-collared day dress of striped fabric,
probably silk, and a cape or cloak, with wide
frilled collar.

Accessories She wears short day gloves,
probably of suede, and holds a long parasol, with
fashionable frilled edge. Her bow-shaped
brooch is probably of paste stones, with a
pendant pearl.

148 The Bayswater Omnibus (detail), 1895
T.M. Joy

Note The businessman wears correct dress for
formal day and city wear.

Head He has very short hair and a heavy
moustache and wears a curly-brimmed top hat.

Body His dress consists of a high starched
winged collar with spotted bow tie; a frock coat
with braided edges; a high-buttoning waistcoat;
and narrow trousers.

Accessories He wears pointed boots and spats
(popular with frock coats from 1893) and has a
metal-framed business bag. The long furled
umbrella was, in this decade, a fashionable
alternative to the cane. A signet ring was now the
only fashionable form of jewellery apart from the
tie-pin. Gloves of fawn kid or grey suede were
usual with frock or morning coats, but he may
have removed them while reading his
newspaper.

149 Fashionable ball dress, 1895
Anon. engraving

Head The women's hairstyles demonstrate a new tendency towards fullness around the face and in the knot at the back, achieved by waving, and sometimes even padding the hair. The only ornaments are perhaps an aigrette or an ornamental comb.

Body Silk dresses feature low-set balloon sleeves, echoing the daytime gigot. Bodices are heavily boned, with pointed waists. Flared skirts have trains, which have to be held up while dancing. The men wear full evening dress, with starched shirts. Lapels are revived for dress coats after 1893.

Accessories The women's long gloves, usually of suede, fasten with up to twenty pearl buttons. Their shoes, usually satin for evening, have very pointed toes and Louis heels. Fans are still very large.

150 Tea-gown, 1895
Anon. engraving

Head The model still wears her hair in the small bun or knot and frizzed fringe of the first half of the 1890s.

Body Her tea-gown is of silk, trimmed with lace. The tea-gown was an easy-fitting, unboned, leisure garment, first introduced in the late 1870s, to give respite from the cuirass bodice of day and evening wear. Initially, it was almost indistinguishable from a dressing-gown, but it became more elaborate in the 1880s, as day wear became more severe. By the late 1880s, it was often worn as an informal dinner dress. Although usually without a waist seam, it always included some fashionable features. Here, the wide yoke, huge gigot sleeves, pointed waistline, and hip-moulding, trained skirt are typical of the mid-1890s.

151 Alfred Austin, 1896
L. Ward

Note The Poet Laureate is in fashionable country clothes.

Head The bowler hat is low crowned and curly-brimmed.

Body He wears a high winged collar, Norfolk jacket and matching knickerbockers, probably of heavy wool tweed. The Norfolk jacket had a distinctive box pleat at the centre back and on each front large patch pockets, concealed vertical breast pocket, and a matching belt, which buttoned at the front waist (those of the 1890s usually had a shoulder yoke). Generally made of thick wool, its warmth and comfortable fit made it ideal for country and sporting wear. It was fashionable throughout the last quarter of the century.

152 **In the holidays, 1897**
Anon. engraving

Note Middle-class families in fashionable but informal seaside wear.

Head Straw sailor hats are popular for men, women and children,
alternatives being soft-peaked caps for men, more dressy wide-brimmed
hats for women, and cotton sunbonnets for little girls (copies of those worn
by countrywomen).

Body and Accessories For women, a tailored jacket, blouse and skirt
(left) are an alternative to day dresses, but both feature high collars, gigot
sleeves, narrow waists and flared skirts. The older girl wears a calf-length
version of adult dress, but the younger ones complement their sunbonnets
with loose, yoked dresses or overalls, based on the country man's smock.
Their brothers wear jerseys and open-legged knickerbockers. Men favour
informal suits and two-tone brogue shoes.

153 Max Beerbohm, 1897
W. Sickert

Note Max Beerbohm wears fashionable casual dress. Shirt collars grew higher in this decade, reaching three inches by 1899. The reefer jacket was distinguished from the lounge by its straight front edges. Originally a yachting coat, it was adopted in the 1860s as a town overcoat. In a shorter, more fitted form, it soon developed as an informal jacket, usually for outdoor wear.

Head He has short hair with a centre parting, a fashionable alternative to the side parting. A clean-shaven face was favoured in 'artistic' circles.

Body and Accessories He has a high standing collar and his spotted silk tie is worn with a 'four-in-hand' or 'Derby' knot, with its distinctive horizontal border along the top and bottom edges. He also wears a high-buttoning waistcoat; a double-breasted reefer jacket; contrasting trousers, probably of flannel; and pointed shoes.

154 The Duchess of Portland in fancy dress, 1897
Anon. photograph

Note Fancy dress balls became increasingly popular during the century. Many outfits revived fashions of previous eras, chosen according to the taste of the day, but however detailed the reconstruction, they always revealed the fashionable features of their own time.

Head and Body Here, the Duchess is dressed for the Devonshire House Ball as the Duchess of Savoy. Her outfit is vaguely 'antique', the pointed waist and hanging sleeves deriving from mediaeval dress, her ringlets, wired neck ruff and jewelled girdle all elements from the sixteenth and seventeenth centuries. Her curved décolletage, puffed sleeves, heavily-boned and fitted bodice and flared skirt are typical of evening dresses in the mid-1890s.

Accessories Pearls were popular in the 1890s as in the seventeenth century.

155 Boulter's Lock, Sunday Afternoon (detail), 1898
E.J. Gregory

Note Middle-class families at leisure on the river.

Head and Body Surprisingly few of the women wear practical blouses and skirts. Most wear more elaborate day dresses and hats. Although several still have full gigot sleeves, the girl in the foreground has adopted the new style, introduced in 1897, featuring narrow sleeves with just a small puff at the shoulder head. Also typical of the late 1890s are the frothy trimmings of lace and frills, particularly half way down the skirt, where they mark a new flare towards the hem. The men generally wear peaked caps, shirts and white flannel trousers. Stripes are popular for caps and blazer jackets.

Accessories Japanese paper sunshades are still a popular accessory.

156 Woman in cycling dress, 1899
B. Partridge

Note The craze for cycling in the 1890s
necessitated more practical styles. Many women
wore a simple blouse, tie and skirt, with sailor
hat. Others ventured divided skirts, and a
minority adopted a wider version of men's
knickerbockers.

Head The woman's hair is waved and padded
and swept into a chignon on top of the head. She
has a low-crowned, curly-brimmed hat, probably
of felt.

Body She wears a scarf or tie in a loose bow; a
tailored jacket, with wide lapels, emphasizing
slightly gathered sleeves; a blouse and perhaps a
waistcoat; and wide knickerbockers. The typical
country man now wears a straw hat, scarf, and
loose informal jacket. He still ties his trousers
with yarks, and wears heavy boots.

Accessories Stockings, high-heeled lace-up
shoes with pointed toes and short gloves are
worn for cycling.

**158 Fashionable walking dress (detail),
1900**
Anon. engraving

Note The emphasis is on height, achieved by
the padded hair and plumed hats, puffed
shoulders, narrow, fitting costumes, and high-
heeled boots and shoes. Nevertheless, padded
busts and hips and heavily-boned, long-fronted
stays create an S-shaped silhouette, completed
by the flowing skirts.

Head The women's hair is rolled and padded
with a knot on top. Their wavy-brimmed hats are
trimmed with feathers, or (left) in ermine to
match the outfit.

Body They wear long fitted pelisses of cloth or
velvet, trimmed with fur; high wired collars;
wide lapels (left); narrow sleeves with small
shoulder puffs; and skirts with short trains, cut
to flare out from below the knee.

Accessories They carry matching muffs with
attached metal-framed purses, decorated with
tassles and a posy of artificial flowers (left).

157 Feminine Pinpricks, 1899
Cleaver

Note The woman in the centre wears a frothy
and undulating day dress in the new style which
appeared from 1897, a reaction against the
severe tailored forms typified by the dresses of
the women in the background.

Head Her hair is rolled and padded to form a
high cushion round the head, topped by a small
knot on the crown. A wide-brimmed hat is tied
with veiling under the chin and she wears a scarf
or jabot of veiling or lace.

Body The dress is of lightweight, clinging silk,
trimmed with lace, frills and bows. Narrow
sleeves, with small puffs at the shoulder and a
pintucked lower sleeve extend over the hand.
The skirt is shaped to fit snugly over the hips,
and then swell out below the knee to a wide hem,
with bias-cut pleats forming a swirling train at
the back.

Select Bibliography

The following publications deal with fashionable dress and accessories. Specific aspects of nineteenth-century dress (e.g. occupational, rural and civic) are dealt with in more general works, and are listed in *Costume: A General Bibliography* by P. Anthony and J. Arnold, published by the Victoria and Albert Museum in association with the Costume Society. Articles and reviews of new material can be found in *Costume,* the annual journal of the Costume Society, and in *Dress,* the journal of the Costume Society of America.

Adburgham, A., *A Punch History of Manners and Modes, 1841-1940,* Hutchinson, 1961

Adburgham, A., Introduction to *Victorian Shopping,* David and Charles, 1972

Adburgham, A., *Shops and Shopping 1800-1914,* Allen and Unwin, 1964 and 1981

Arnold, J., *Patterns of Fashion I (c. 1660-1860)* and *II (1860-1940),* Wace, 1964, Macmillan 1972

Blum, S. (ed.), *Victorian Fashions and Costumes from Harper's Bazaar 1867-1898,* Dover, New York, 1974

Blum, S. (ed.), *Ackermann's Costume Plates: Women's Fashions in England 1818-1828,* Dover, New York, 1978

Buck, A., Victorian Costume and Costume Accessories, Herbert Jenkins, 1961

Buck, A., 'The Costume of Jane Austen and her Characters' in *The So-called Age of Elegance,* The Costume Society, 1970

Buck, A., 'The Trap Rebaited, Mourning Dress 1860-1890' in *High Victorian,* The Costume Society, 1968

Byrde, P., *The Male Image: Men's Fashion in England 1300-1970,* Batsford, 1979

Byrde, P., *A Frivolous Distinction: Fashion and Needlework in the Works of Jane Austen,* Bath City Council, 1979

Clark, F., *Hats,* Batsford, 1982

Cunnington, C.W., *English Women's Clothing in the Nineteenth Century,* Faber, 1937

Cunnington, C.W. and P., *The History of Underclothes,* Faber, 1951, revised 1981

Cunnington, C.W. and P., *Handbook of English Costume in the Nineteenth Century,* Faber, 1959 and 1970

Evans, J., *A History of Jewellery 1100-1870,* Faber, 1953 and 1970

Flower, M., *Victorian Jewellery,* Cassell, 1951

Foster, V., *Bags and Purses,* Batsford, 1982

Gernsheim, A., *Fashion and Reality 1840-1914,* Faber 1963, reprinted as *Victorian and Edwardian Fashion: A Photographic Survey,* Dover, New York, 1981

Gibbs-Smitt, C., *The Fashionable Lady in the Nineteenth Century,* H.M.S.O., 1960

Ginsburg, M., *An Introduction to Fashion Illustration,* Victoria and Albert Museum, 1980

Ginsburg, M., *Victorian Dress in Photographs,* Batsford, 1982

Holland, V., *Hand-Coloured Fashion Plates 1770-1899,* London, 1955

Hope, T. and Moses, H., *Designs of Modern Costume Engraved for Thomas Hope of Deepdene by Henry Moses, 1812,* Introduction by J.L. Nevinson, Costume Society Extra Series no. 4, 1973

Irwin, J., *Shawls,* H.M.S.O., 1955

'A Lady', *The Workwoman's Guide,* 1838, reprinted by Bloomfield Books, Doncaster, 1975

Laver, J. (introduction), *Costume Illustration: The Nineteenth Century,* H.M.S.O., 1947

Manchester City Art Galleries, *Women's Costume 1800-35,* Manchester City Art Gallery, 1952

Manchester City Art Galleries, *Women's Costume 1835-70,* Manchester City Art Gallery, 1951

Manchester City Art Galleries, *Women's Costume 1870-1900,* Manchester City Art Gallery, 1953

Moore, D.L., *Fashion Through Fashion Plates 1771-1970,* London, 1965

Newton, S.M., *Health, Art and Reason, Dress Reformers of the Nineteenth Century,* John Murray, 1974

Rhead, G.W., *History of the Fan,* K. Paul, 1910

Rock, C.H., *Paisley Shawls,* Paisley Museum and Art

Galleries, 1966

Swann, J., *Shoes*, Batsford, 1982

Walkley, C., *The Ghost in the Looking Glass: The Victorian Seamstress*, Peter Owen, 1981

Walkley, C., and Foster, V., *Crinolines and Crimping Irons; Victorian Clothes: How They Were Cleaned and Cared For*, Peter Owen, 1978

Waugh, N., *The Cut of Men's Clothes 1600-1900*, Faber, 1964

Waugh, N., *The Cut of Women's Clothes 1600-1930*, Faber, 1968

Waugh, N., *Corsets and Crinolines*, Batsford, 1954 and 1972

Glossary and Select Index

Note This lists costume and textile terms mentioned in the captions, with a definition where this is not included in either text or caption. The numbers in brackets refer to plates where selected examples of the item listed can be studied. (Basic garments such as *bonnets, shawls, top hats* etc. appear too frequently to be included in this system.)

Aesthetic dress (125) (127) (128)

Aigrette a tuft usually of feathers, but sometimes of flowers or jewels. (149)

Apollo knot a knot of hair on the crown of the head, topped by vertical loops of stiffened, plaited hair, often secured by Glauvina pins (q.v.). (40) (42) (46)

Basques tab-like extensions below the waist of a bodice. (69) (109)

Bavolet a curtain of fabric attached to the back of a bonnet to shade the neck. (61)

Bedgown a short, loose, wrap-over gown, often worn as a jacket by country women. (16)

Beret sleeve a short, very wide, puffed sleeve. (46) (47)

Bertha a deep collar falling as a continuous band from a low neckline. (51) (60) (66)

Bishop sleeve a long, full sleeve, gathered to the wrist. (86) (91)

Blazer a flannel sports jacket with patch pockets. Usually striped or brightly coloured, hence the name. (155)

Blonde lace made from undyed silk. (41) (42)

Bloomer dress (69)

Blouse (144)

Blucher boots men's half boots with straight tops and front lacing. (79)

Boater see *Sailor hat.*

Bobbin lace an openwork mesh made by interweaving threads wound on bobbins. (68) (87)

Bowler a hard felt hat with a bowl-shaped crown and curled brim. Called a Derby in the USA. (100) (124) (151)

Breeches (1) (68) (128)

Brocade a woven fabric, with elaborate patterns created by the introduction of additional threads of a different yarn or colour. (54) (108)

Broderie anglaise coarse, openwork embroidery, the large holes overcast with stitching. (75) (83)

Bullycock (Billycock) hat (52)

Burnous mantle a loose form of mantle with a tasselled hood. (84)

Busk a flat rod, inserted into the front of a corset to stiffen it. It was usually made of wood or whalebone in the early part of the century, and of metal from the 1860s. (14)

Bustle (2) (24) (40) (109) (130)

Cape a short cloak. (146)

Chapeau bras a crescent-shaped opera hat, which could be folded flat. (11)

Chatelaine a metal waist ornament with attached chains from which were suspended domestic accessories (e.g. keys, scissors, scent-bottle). (141)

Chatelaine bag a bag hung from the waist. (122)

Chemise a female undergarment consisting of a long, loose, low-necked, short-sleeved shirt, worn next to the skin. It was made of linen or cotton. (14) (40)

Chemisette in the first half of the century, a high-necked, sleeveless muslin half-shirt, worn as a fill-in for low-necked dresses; by the 1860s, a long-sleeved blouse. (14) (25) (32)

Chenille a furry looking silk thread with a long pile. (86)

Chesterfield overcoat (140)

Clocks patterned areas on stockings in the region of the ankle. (14)

Cornette a bonnet-shaped cap, tying beneath the chin. It was sometimes pointed at the back. (14)

Court dress (28) (87)

Crinoline a petticoat distended by hoops of cane, whalebone or steel, introduced in 1856. (85) (88) (96) (98)

Cuirass bodice a heavily whaleboned bodice, extending over the hips in a point front and back. It was named after a form of body armour. (109) (120)

Damask a heavy woven cloth with a reversible pattern produced by alternating plain and satin weaves. (65)

Dandies (9) (24) (36) (43) (58)

Disposition, à a term applied in the 1850s to ready-patterned skirt flounces. (75) (78)

Drawers (14) (47) (60)

Dress coat a man's formal tail coat, cut square across the waist. (19)

Dressing gown (20) (119)

Epaulette an ornamental shoulder-piece in the form of a short cap to the top of the sleeve. (92)

Falls a form of closure for trousers, breeches, and pantaloons, by means of a falling flap at the front, which buttoned to the waist. (1)

Fichu-pelerine a pelerine (q.v.) with scarf-like extensions hanging down at the front. (44) (45)

Figured fabric a fabric woven with a pattern, but without additional threads of a different yarn or colour (compare *Brocade*). (54) (65)

Frock coat a man's skirted coat of about knee length, characterized by its straight front edges. (21) (24) (26) (105)

Gaiters protective leggings fastening with buttons or straps and extending over the foot. (52)

Gaiter bottoms a term applied to trouser bottoms where the side seams curve forward, producing a flared front to accommodate the foot. (58)

Gauging a technique of gathering skirts, by which the fabric is finely pleated, together with its lining, and sewn to the bodice at alternate pleats. (63)

Gigot ('leg-of-mutton') sleeves sleeves with very full puffed shoulders, but tapering to a narrow wrist. (36) (38) (48) (146)

Glauvina ('Glorvina') pins ornamental hair pins with detachable heads. (See *Apollo knot*).

Gore a triangular-shaped panel in a skirt, adding width at the hem, without fullness at the waist. (97) (145)

Half boots short boots, reaching just above the ankle.

Hessian boot a knee-length boot with a heart-shaped peak at the front, often decorated with a tassel in the centre. (4) (9) (19) (23)

Jabot an ornamental frill on the front of the bodice. (122) (126)

Jersey a knitted top, originally worn by sailors, but adopted by women and children in the 1880s. (80) (152)

Knickerbockers baggy breeches, usually gathered just below the knee. (119) (151) (156)

Lappets long bands attached to a cap or headdress and hanging down over the ears. (28)

Louis heels strictly a heel continuous with the sole, but used to describe a curved heel, set well under the foot, as found in eighteenth-century French shoes. (149)

Lounge jacket a short jacket, worn informally. When accompanied by matching waistcoat and trousers, it became a lounge suit. (91) (145)

M-notch lapel an M-shaped opening at the join of collar and lapel, found in men's coats between 1800 and 1855 (and in evening coats until the 1870s). (9) (10) (19)

Mancheron a short, flat oversleeve. (5) (17) (49)

Mantle at the beginning of the period, a cape with scarf-like extensions; by the 1820s it had become a loose-fitting wrap, half way between a coat and a cloak, with wide sleeves or armhole slits. There were many individually named variations. (2) (59) (69) (138)

Marie Stuart bonnet or cap a cap cut with a distinctive dip in the centre front, imitating the heart-shaped caps worn by Mary Queen of Scots. (33) (35)

Mentonnière ('chin stays') a ruffle of tulle or lace at the top of bonnet strings creating a frill around the chin. (50)

Mittens (48) (54)

Mourning coat a tail coat with curved front edges. Originally a riding coat worn in the morning, it became general day wear. (6) (34) (43) (81)

Morning dress (96) (97)

Mousquetaire hat a low-crowned, wide-brimmed hat with a feather plume, inspired by those of seventeenth-century musketeers. (78)

Norfolk suit (151)

Pagoda sleeve a sleeve which was tight to the upper arm and flaring below the elbow. It became very wide between the years 1857 and 1860. (78) (83)

Paletot the French term for overcoat, it was applied in the mid-century to short loose coats, usually without a waist seam. (88) (90)

Pannier part of a skirt or overskirt which is looped up in a puff on the hips. (108) (129)

Pantaloons a form of very tight-fitting legwear, usually made of stretchy fabric or soft leather. (6) (9) (19) (36)

Patent leather a very glossy leather made from hide coated with layers of varnish or lacquer.

Peg-top (usually applied to sleeves or trousers) cut wide at the top and tapering towards the bottom.

Pelerine a very wide, cape-like collar. (41) (44) (48) (56)

Pelisse a woman's fitted overcoat. (5) (15) (18) (45) (158)

Pelisse dress a dress cut in imitation of a pelisse (e.g. with lapels and/or a belt) popular in the late 1830s and 1840s. (50)

Pinking the raw edge of fabric cut in zigzags or scallops. (78)

Piping the insertion of a fabric-covered cord into a seam to stiffen it, the tube of fabric being all that is visible. (61) (63)

Plastron a loose panel of fabric inserted down the centre front of a bodice, creating the effect of a waistcoat. (129) (130)

Pointing decorative lines of stitching on the backs of gloves. (140)

Polonaise a bodice with attached overskirt. An eighteenth-century form, revived from the mid-1860s onwards. Those of the late 1870s were so long as to be almost indistinguishable from a dress. (103) (118) (122)

Pork-pie hat a small round hat with an upturned brim almost flush with the crown. (88)

Post-boy hat (136)

Princess dress a style of dress without a waist seam, perhaps called after Princess Alexandra. (121) (122)

Pump a light shoe, usually low-cut, with flat or low heel. (23)

Reefer an informal jacket, usually double-breasted and with straight front edges, derived from a yachting coat. (153)

Reticule an early form of handbag, usually in the form of a simple rectangle of fabric fastened with a drawstring. (24) (45) (52) (140)

Rouleau a trimming consisting of a puffed or padded roll of fabric. (31) (39)

Sailor hat a low-crowned, narrow-brimmed straw hat. (144) (152)

Sandal a flat shoe with ribbon ties around the ankle. (15) (22) (40)

Sevigné bodice a bodice decorated with horizontal pleats caught by a vertical band in the centre. It was named after the Marquise de Sevigné (1626-96). (46)

Shawl collar a collar continuous with the lapels. (43)

Smock (52) (68)

Smoking cap (123)

Spats short gaiters, reaching just above the ankle. (148)

Spencer a woman's short-waisted, long-sleeved jacket. (16) (21) (31)

Spoon bonnet a small bonnet with sloping brim and cut-away sides, creating a spoon shape. (89) (93)

Stays (14) (40)

Stock a made-up, stiffened neck band, fastening behind, with or without a bow in front. (6) (34)

Stocking purse a tubular purse of knitted silk or cotton, the coins being inserted through a slit in the middle and secured in the ends by metal rings. (78)

Stomacher a panel of fabric, in the shape of an inverted triangle, inserted between the centre front edges of the bodice. Popular in the seventeenth and eighteenth centuries it was often imitated in the nineteenth. (28) (120)

Sunbonnet a bonnet with a very deep bavolet (q.v.), worn by country women to protect them from the sun. It was usually made of printed cotton gathered on to half hoops of cane or whalebone. (152)

Swiss belt a wide belt with a double point centre front. (92)

Tablier, en lines of trimming on a skirt front arranged in an inverted 'V' to imitate a front opening. (50)

Tail coat see *Dress coat* and *Morning coat.*

Tea-gown (150)

Tie-back skirt a skirt made with internal tapes passing between the side seams at the back, so that the fabric is drawn closely to the hips and legs at the front, and the fullness concentrated at the back, usually in a train. (118) (120) (121)

Titus, à la a term applied to hair worn short and tousled, in the style of the Roman emperor of that name. (1) (2)

Toe spring the elevation of the toe of a shoe above the ground. (81)

Top boot a tall boot with the top turned down to show the paler lining. (24)

Top frock an overcoat in the style of a frock coat, but usually with wider lapels and cuffs. (105)

Toque a hat, usually small, with little or no turned-up brim. (44) (126) (140)

Tucker a frill of muslin or lace worn inside a low neckline. (The term was sometimes applied to a more substantial fill-in.) (27) (66)

Ugly a folding sunshade worn at the front of a bonnet, and consisting of a band of silk (usually blue) distended by half hoops of cane. (73)

Ulster (111)

Undersleeves (62) (83)

Vamp the front part of a shoe upper, covering the toes and part of the instep. (15) (20)

Vandyking zigzag edgings, supposedly imitating the pointed lace collars and cuffs of the seventeenth century, as depicted in portraits by Van Dyck. (29) (39) (42) (120)

Victoria sleeve a sleeve puffed at the elbow (49) (59)

Warp-printing the printing of warp threads of a fabric before weaving to produce a blurred pattern. (72)

Watered silk – (moiré antique) a corded silk pressed between heated rollers so that the crushed cords reflect the light in wave-like patterns. (55) (99)

Wideawake hat (71)

Winged collar a standing collar with the two front points turned down. (135)

Yark a cord used by country men and labourers to hitch up their baggy trousers below the knee. (79) (156)